LOVE THAT LASTS

MAKING A MAGNIFICENT MARRIAGE

GARY AND BETSY RICUCCI

SERIES EDITOR: GREG SOMERVILLE

PEOPLE OF DESTINY
INTERNATIONAL

People of Destiny International serves a growing network
of local churches in the United States and abroad.
For information about the ministry or for permission
to reproduce portions of this book, contact:

People of Destiny International
7881 Beechcraft Avenue, Suite B
Gaithersburg, MD 20879

Authors: Gary and Betsy Ricucci
Cover design by Gallison Design
Book layout by Beth Kelley

ISBN 1-881039-02-1

Printed in the United States of America

CONTENTS

FOREWORD

With every page of this book, we've had to humbly and gratefully ask ourselves, "And what do you have that you did not receive?" (1Co 4:7). We didn't write this book as marriage experts, but as a couple to whom God has been very gracious. He has set us in a church where Jesus Christ and his Word are pre-eminent, and marriages and families are a top priority. And within Covenant Life Church he has surrounded us with friends, examples, instruction, care, accountability, and encouragement.

We have developed this material with two objectives in mind: changed lives and transformed marriages. This doesn't mean marriage is an end in itself. God's best is a marriage that reflects the glorious union between Christ and his Church; a marriage that contributes to the Lord's purpose of building his Church and preparing the next generation; and a marriage that offers hope and help to families desperate for answers. We trust that our efforts will inspire faith, and will instill in you a determination to take whatever steps necessary to build such a marriage.

For some, reading this book may be part of a painful search for a glimmer of hope. For others, you're still engulfed in the afterglow of your honeymoon. And most of the couples reading this book simply want to take a next step toward a truly wonderful and magnificent marriage. Though each situation is different, God will always honor faith and obedience, because he is faithful and his Word is true.

To those who have given so generously to make this book a reality we want to express specific thanks. The actual writing and editorial process was meticulously overseen by Greg Somerville, whose many talents have made this material so readily applicable. Thanks as well to production coordinator Beth Kelley who put all the pieces together in a timely and readable fashion.

To those fellow leaders and many authors who allowed us to present or adapt their material, we say thank you, not only for your kindness but for the fruit we've seen in our own marriage as a result of your instruction. We are indebted as well to our friends, the pastors of Covenant Life Church and their wives, for their encouragement and support as we wrote.

We also want to commend the couples, families, and leaders in the Family Life Ministries of Covenant Life Church. Your commitment to be not only hearers but doers of God's Word makes serving you, and serving with you, such a joy!

And finally, special thanks and appreciation to our heroes—Covenant Life Church's senior pastor, C.J. Mahaney, and his wife Carolyn. Your wisdom, example, and instruction are reflected throughout this book, and your affirmation and confidence in us for this project has meant so much. Your passion for Jesus Christ and his Church; your love for one another and your family; and your friendship, care, and leadership are among God's greatest gifts to us.

—Gary and Betsy Ricucci

HOW TO USE THIS BOOK

Love That Lasts is part of a series of books designed for group and individual study. The series is the logical outgrowth of four deeply held convictions:

■ The Bible is our infallible standard for faith, doctrine, and practice. Unless we yield to its authority, we will be blown off course by our own emotions and cultural pressures.

■ Knowledge without application is lifeless. God's Word has to be applied before we can be transformed. Truth doesn't change us until we practice it in daily life.

■ Application of these principles is impossible without dependence upon the Holy Spirit. While we must participate in change, he is the source of our power.

■ The church is God's intended context for change. God never intended for us to live isolated or independent of other Christians.Through committed participation in the local church, we can receive instruction, encouragement, correction, and opportunities to press on toward maturity in Christ.

As you work through these pages, we trust that each of these foundational convictions will be reinforced in your own heart.

With the possible exception of the "Group Discussion" questions, the format of this book is equally suited for individuals and small groups. A variety of different elements have been included to make each study as interesting and relevant as possible.

Scripture Context: Begin by going to the source.

Warm-Up: A little mental exercise to get you in the mood.

Personal Study: Here is the meat of the lesson, spiced with occasional questions to help you apply what you're reading.

Margin Questions: If you have the time, dig deeper into the lesson as you *Meditate On...* biblical truths or turn to related passages *For Further Study*.

Group Discussion: Though you may not get past the first question or two, these are guaranteed to get your group thinking and talking about real-life issues.

Recommended Reading: For those who can't get enough of a particular topic, here's a whole bookshelf full of great resources.

While you are encouraged to experiment in your use of this book, group discussion will be better served when members work through the material in advance. And remember that you're not going through this book alone. The Holy Spirit is your tutor. With his help, these studies may well change your life.

—**Greg Somerville**, *Series Editor*

TILL DEATH DO US PART

GARY AND BETSY RICUCCI

SCRIPTURE TEXT Genesis 2:19-24

WARM-UP Which of the following comes closest to describing your primary motivation for getting married?[1]

❑ Fell in love

❑ Fear of loneliness or rejection

❑ Security

❑ Sexual desire

❑ Money or prestige

❑ Everybody just expected we would get married

❑ Premarital pregnancy left little choice

❑ Sensed a call from God

❑ It just seemed like the right thing to do

PERSONAL STUDY There are at least three possible reasons which could explain why you have begun reading this book:

■ Your spouse gave it to you as a birthday present and your exceptional powers of discernment said, "This is a clue!"

■ Your small group leader assigned it and asked you to lead the discussion at the next meeting

■ You genuinely want to improve your marriage

Whatever the reasons, we believe you are going to enjoy working through this book. It offers biblical truths and practical illustrations which, when properly applied in a context of support and accountability, will help make your marriage magnificent in the truest sense of the word. And that's why we've put this material in print. Over the past number of years we have seen scores of couples study and apply these principles with far-reaching effects. There's no reason to believe it will have any less impact on you.

At the outset, we want to point out three fundamental attitudes that will determine how much—or how little—you benefit from this study book. Lasting change in your marriage will depend on...

■ A **conviction** that the Lord Jesus Christ and his Word provide the foundation for marriage. This is the only foundation on which a lasting and magnificent marriage can be built.

■ A **confidence** in God's faithfulness and his involvement in your marriage. Is it possible for a wife to submit to her husband as to the Lord, or for a husband to love his wife as Christ loved the Church (Eph 5:22,25)? Yes it is—but not without divine assistance. Apart from the active grace of God working in us we have no hope of being able to love each other the way God intends.

■ A **commitment** to humbly and wholeheartedly seek change, even when it's awkward, difficult, or demanding. Pleasing God through consistent growth and change should be our life's ambition.

A few other ground rules before we get into the heart of this study. First, each of us needs to assume personal responsibility for what God is saying to us. It's not the husband's job to supervise his wife's progress through this study, or vice versa. The Holy Spirit fills that role perfectly. Besides, we've got our hands full with ourselves!

Second, we want to avoid stereotypes throughout this book. Every woman and man is different, and consequently no two marriages are the same. Situations and circumstances—and therefore applications—vary widely. Our goal is to communicate what God has clearly revealed through his Word for husbands and wives regardless of culture, circumstance, or season of life.

Third, recognize that marriage is a context for discipleship. The same guidelines we practice as servants of Jesus Christ—like forsaking all to follow him, forgiving seventy times seven, or developing the fruit of the Spirit—apply to and strengthen our marriages. In fact, if we consistently obeyed the Bible as it relates to being a disciple of Jesus,

> **❝** I have never been given to envy, save for the envy I feel toward those people who have the ability to make a marriage work and endure happily. It's an art I have never seemed able to master. My record? Five marriages, five divorces. In short—five failures. **❞**
>
> —**Billionaire J. Paul Getty**

Meditate on Romans 15:7 and 14:4. What is your primary duty toward your spouse? What is God's duty toward him/her?

4

we wouldn't need much of this study book. As we love and obey Jesus, allowing his Spirit to change us, he will work wonders in our marriages.

Our hope is that this book will ignite a desire in your heart for a great marriage—a *magnificent* marriage. By the power of God, coupled with your faith and obedience, it can be done!

---

1 What three qualities do you want to characterize your marriage?

-
-
-

A Word to Christian Women

Without healthy marriages, there would be no healthy society. Yet a biblically based marriage flies right in the face of popular culture. The challenge is probably most difficult for the Christian woman. How does the world define success for her? A career, an independent income, a lavishly furnished house, a new car, a stylish wardrobe, and perhaps a graduate degree or two. What of the fact that she does a masterful job of stretching her husband's income and joyfully supports him in his calling? That means little to the world. If she lives in a rented apartment, drives a well-worn car, and doesn't have a "real job," today's culture would give her no affirmation or applause.

Contrary to popular opinion, woman was not created for her own fulfillment. (That goes for the men, too!) She was created to be a helper and a nurturer. Now that is not an easy assignment to accept. We tend to bristle and think, *There must be something more significant than that!* What homemaker hasn't found herself asking, after the fiftieth load of laundry in a week or when facing yet another sink full of dirty dishes, "Is there anything significant about what I'm doing here?" Yet in God's eyes, nothing is more significant than servanthood. The path to genuine greatness lies in serving.

Meditate on Matthew 20:25-28. How does God define significance?

Grasping for power or recognition is natural. Servant-hood is supernatural. So many women are missing out on the supernatural today because they are caught up in the "search for significance." Ironically, the more they search for it, the less satisfied they feel. Why? Significance is found in giving your life away, not in selfishly trying to find personal happiness.

Television commercials would have us believe there are only two kinds of wives: the dull-witted slave, whose greatest thrill in life is finding a toilet-bowl cleaner that really works, or the independent, self-fulfilled career woman with everything under control. Both are illusions. The first one mocks us; the second one misleads us. Too many women have reached for that golden thread of self-reliance and material-ism, thinking it will satisfy, only to realize that instead of finding treasure at the end of that thread they're seeing the fabric of society unravel before their very eyes.

> 66 Wives and mothers can evaluate their vision and values by answering the question, 'Twenty years from now, what will I wish I had done today?' Few women envision themselves sitting in the rocker reflecting on a history of clean bathrooms, or a sterling career, at the expense of their husband or their children.[2] 99
>
> —Jean Fleming

Proverbs 31 honors another kind of wife, one whose character is noble, who fears the Lord, and whose multiple vocations include businesswoman, interior designer, personnel manager, teacher, and everything in between! And running a home requires every one of these! Derek Kidner describes the Proverbs 31 wife as showing "the fullest flowering of domesticity, which is revealed as no petty and restricted sphere, and its mistress as no cipher. Here is scope for formidable powers and great achievements...."[3] (Like the sound of that, ladies?)

But it's how she uses her formidable powers and great achievements that is most impressive. Not for material gain, professional accolades, or personal gratification—she pours them out before her Lord in service to her husband, children, family, church, and community.

Here is the real success story. As she rises to the super-natural, choosing to serve her husband, build her home, and prepare the next generation, the Christian wife will be doing the most significant thing she possibly could with her life. The world may still mock, but God will consider her great. (And if he is the least bit perceptive, so will her husband!)

A Stronger Word to Christian Men

Husbands, before you start leaving highlighted copies of the previous section around the house as a reminder to your wives, it would be well worth your while to sit down and open your Bible to Ephesians 5:25-29:

> Husbands, love your wives, just as Christ loved the church and gave himself up for her to make her holy, cleansing her by the washing with water through the word, and to present her to himself as a radiant church, without stain or wrinkle or any other blemish, but holy and blameless. In this same way, husbands ought to love their wives as their own bodies. He who loves his wife loves himself. After all, no one ever hated his own body, but he feeds and cares for it, just as Christ does the church...

Women who react against the call to submission are often the ones who have yet to see this passage consistently and practically applied. Men, if we want the kind of radiant bride described here, we must begin by paying the same radical price.

Message sent. Message received?

What Is Marriage?

Because of its biblical illiteracy, our society struggles to come up with a clear definition of marriage and family, as the White House "Conference on the Family" proved several years ago. Their task was to answer the question, "What is a family?" One hundred years ago that question would have seemed absurd. But not now, when no-fault divorce and the sexual revolution have cluttered the family tree with multiple parents, half-siblings, gay lovers, and "significant others." The conference participants eventually concluded that a family is all the people living in the same house. Presumably that would include a college fraternity house. That's frightening. It's also destructively inaccurate.

The meaning of marriage is equally endangered. Fortunately we don't need to tailor our definition to suit opinion polls, lobbyists, or "experts." God's Word clearly describes what a marriage is and is not. You don't have to read far in the Bible to be astounded by God's perspective on this most sacred and significant relationship.

Marriage is the first institution (Ge 2:22-24). It was ordained before the family, before civil government—even before the Church.

Marriage depicts the supernatural union between Jesus and the Church (Eph 5:31-32). One of the most beautiful analogies God uses to define his relationship with us is that of a marriage. To grasp this is both inspiring and sobering. People should be able to look at our marriages and say, "So that's what the Church is like? That's what it means to have a relationship with Jesus?" Most of us are so aware of the deficiencies in our marriages that the comparison makes us uncomfortable. Yet God wouldn't have used the analogy if it weren't possible. It's overwhelming to realize he intends to cultivate the same abundant, unconditional love between a husband and wife as he himself has for us. Marriage is a profound and marvelous mystery established by God for his glory.

For Further Study:
Calling it a "profound mystery," Paul compared marriage to the relationship between Christ and the Church. To better understand this mystery, look up these verses: Isa 62:5, Jer 2:2, Jn 3:29, Rev 19:7, 21:2, and 21:9.

---

2 Imagine your pastor calls you tomorrow evening and says, "As part of our effort to communicate what it means to know Jesus, we've been videotaping your marriage all week. It will be on the air this coming Friday!"

Christ's reputation is at stake. Are there any scenes from this past week you would want to edit?

Marriage is the event God has selected to consummate all of time (Rev 19:7). God has had at least 2,000 years to make preparations for honoring his Son at the end of the age. It's significant that God has not scheduled the coronation of the Lamb or the graduation of the Lamb. Instead he has ordained the marriage supper of the Lamb. Why marriage? Because it speaks of union and intimacy and fruitfulness like nothing else does. The greatest thing God could plan for Jesus was to present him with his radiant Bride. No wonder we are so deeply moved when a bride walks down the aisle. Marriage is a holy and wonderful gift. And one day we will be called to account for our stewardship of this gift.

Marriage is to be held in honor (Heb 13:4). The Amplified Version of the Bible elaborates on this verse, noting that marriage should be esteemed worthy, precious, of great price, and especially dear. This requires that we guard against any thought, attitude, word, or action that dishonors or belittles our spouse or marriage. It's hard enough to squelch our own selfishness and insensitivity; throw in the media's steady bombardment of marriage-bashing and we have our work cut out for us.

When I (Gary) stop at the grocery store for milk and bread, I will often buy flowers for Betsy. On one particular trip, when I reached the cashier, he joked, "What's the matter—you in the doghouse?" It would have been easy to laugh along with him and join in the joke. But I wanted him to know my marriage was important to me. Here was a chance to challenge his misconception, to sow in his mind a seed of hope about the tremendous potential of marriage. So without getting self-righteous about it, I answered, "No—I just love my wife."

Your spouse is created in the image of God. Your marriage is a sacred relationship. Keep that in mind next time you're at a family or social gathering and the familiar jokes start flying. You'll need to use wisdom here. It probably won't help matters if you turn your Thanksgiving dinner blessing into a sermon on the virtues of marriage. But look for some way to communicate that you *enjoy* being married, that God is in it. Use every opportunity to defend the sanctity of marriage.

One way we can honor marriage is by refusing to dishonor our marriage partner. Betsy and I have a great relationship. We enjoy joking with each other, and often we laugh at each other, but I won't belittle or intentionally embarrass her in front of others. And I don't compare her unfavorably with anyone. That's a vow I made and have kept since our wedding day.

Marriage is much more than a ceremony. A wedding is an event, but a marriage is a state of being. It's not a one-time act; it's a lifelong commitment to be developed and maintained. Marriage is a continuous quest to know your mate and to become one flesh.

Marriage is a refining process. Conflict occurs in every marriage. When issues erupt between husband and wife, it's easy for one to blame the other. "If you would just leave the air conditioner on when it gets this hot, I wouldn't get

Meditate on Colossians 4:5-6.
What opportunities do you have to confront, in a gracious way, society's distorted view of marriage?

> ❝ One thing the world will not do is give your marriage a priority position in life. If your relationship is esteemed, it is because you have made it so. If it is prized, it is because you prize it. If you and your mate have had the desperately needed time to interact with one another in a meaningful manner, it is not because our culture decided to give it to you. It is because you took it.[4] ❞
>
> **—Donald R. Harvey**

9

upset!" The fact is, our spouses don't make us sin. They simply reveal what's already in our heart. You may not appreciate it, but one of the best wedding gifts God gave you was a full-length mirror called your spouse. Had there been a card attached, it would have said, "Here's to helping you discover what you're *really* like. Congratulations!"

---

3 Write down two or three of the blemishes you've discovered in yourself thanks to your marital mirror:

-

-

-

Camouflaging selfishness can be simpler when you're single, but it's impossible when you're married. Don't waste the energy trying. Instead, recognize the bondage that selfishness brings, and thank God for using your spouse to reveal it. When we come face to face with our self-centered sins, God says, "You don't have to be bound by that anger, that impatience, that lust, covetousness, and materialism. I can free you from that if you will obey me and then serve your spouse." As the Lord, through our repentance, sets us free from selfishness, we are then free to serve him and our spouse with gladness.

If you're reading this and you're not yet married, don't misunderstand what we're saying. Marriage is not one continual, raging fire of confrontation and refinement. Serious conflicts are the exception in a healthy marriage. But if we're wise, we can insure that even the conflicts are ultimately constructive.

Marriage is not an end in itself. Marriage is to fulfill God's purpose in building his Church, preparing the next generation, and testifying to the world of the peace and order of his kingdom. A satisfying marriage can become an idol if it's the goal rather than the result of faith-filled serving and obedience.

As we wrap up our definition of marriage, the following four visual images may help clarify what we've discussed:

■ Marriage is a **plumb line.** When a husband and wife remain true to God's Word, their life and love provide an accurate measure of where the culture actually lines up with God's standard.

■ Marriage is an **anchor.** When you refuse to drift with the latest fad or marital trend, people notice. We've had people ask us, "Are you guys still having fun?" Beneath their light-hearted question is a note of desperation. They want to know whether marriage can really work. They want to know there is something they can believe in. It's a joy to answer, "Yes! Marriage takes lots of work, but the dividends are worth all the investment...and we're having a great time!"

■ Marriage is a **lifeboat.** All around you are couples who need help. A godly marriage offers tremendous hope to husbands and wives in need of answers and solutions.

■ Marriage is a **blueprint.** The greatest compliment I (Betsy) have ever received is hearing my daughters say, "When I grow up, I want to be a wife and a mom, too." Our efforts to build a magnificent marriage don't only result in a deep sense of personal fulfillment; we are giving substance and direction to the generations to come.

Serious Business

On the day a man and woman say to each other, "I do," something takes place which is not only legal and relational, but supernatural. In the presence of God and his people, this couple totally and irrevocably commit to serve and love each other in full obedience to God's Word. They enter a covenant.

> **"** Marriage is a covenant, a vow. In the Bible, covenants are never private. It is one thing for a young man to whisper promises to a young woman in a private, romantic setting; it is quite another to pledge a vow publicly in front of witnesses. The public nature of the covenant forces the couple to face the full responsibility of marriage.[5] **"**
> —R.C. Sproul

The word "covenant" is not in vogue today, and its meaning is poorly understood. A covenant is more than a promise, more than a pledge, more than a vow. It is a formal, solemn, binding agreement and union. Entering into a covenant with someone has vast implications and necessitates the utmost commitment. When the Israelites asked God why he no longer responded to their prayers, he gave them this answer through the prophet Malachi: "It is because the Lord is acting as the witness between you and the wife of your youth, because you have broken faith with her, though she is your partner, the wife of your marriage covenant" (Mal 2:14). Breaking a covenant is serious business. Ecclesiastes 5:4-5 goes so far as to warn us that it's better never to vow than to make a vow and not fulfill it.

God created covenant as his means of relating to us. He made a covenant with Noah (Ge 6:17-19); with Abraham (Ge 15:18); with Moses (Ex 34:10); and with David (2Ch 21:7). Through the person and work of Jesus Christ he has entered into a covenant with us (Mt 26:27-28; Heb 8). Covenant is a sacred treasure in the heart of God. Our reverence for God should lead us to esteem what he esteems, and to honor the covenant of marriage with all diligence.

Covenant requires sacrifice, as the relationship between Jonathan and David so beautifully illustrates. Although he put himself at risk because of King Saul's eventual hatred for David, "Jonathan made a covenant with David because he loved him as himself" (1Sa 18:3; 20:32-42).

Covenant also requires death. Under the old covenant that involved animal sacrifice; the new covenant was ratified by the blood of Christ. In the same way, to experience the benefit of our marriage covenant we must be prepared to lay down our lives. Not that we are forced to crucify our personality or calling, but anything that competes or interferes with our covenant has to go. It's the seemingly harmless things—the "little foxes," as Solomon called them (SS 2:15)—that so often ruin a marriage.

Meditate on Psalm 25:14. Our fear of God enables us to understand the significance of covenant love.

Living in God's kingdom means doing the exact opposite of our selfish and sinful instincts. If you want to get, you give. In order to gain your life, you lose it. The extent to which we are willing to sacrifice for our spouse is the extent to which we will have life and joy in that relationship. Covenant has a cost. Just look at the cross.

4 Pause here for a minute and ask God to show you areas you may need to sacrifice for the good of your marriage (like a hobby, overtime at work, TV, or projects). Record your impressions in the space below.

Covenant is more than a partnership—it's a union. The difference is profound. Marriage takes two people and turns them into one new being. Though each has a separate identity and personality, they have been joined. What affects one will affect the other. This is why divorce is so traumatic—it shreds a couple's oneness. God is powerful enough to restore those who have gone through divorce and gracious enough to forgive, yet Scripture pulls no punches in expressing God's attitude toward divorce: he hates it (Mal 2:16). Scripture seems to give only two instances where divorce and remarriage are legitimate: 1) If the spouse is an adulterer, and 2)If the spouse leaves, abandoning his or her partner.

Our union in marriage closely resembles our union with Christ. God's Spirit indwells us. Christ is in us (Col 1:27). "He who unites himself with the Lord is one with him in spirit" (1Co 6:17). What a mystery! We don't become God, and God doesn't become a man, but we are joined in a way meant to be eternal and unbreakable. In a similarly mysterious and wonderful way we become one with our spouse. We may never fully understand the marriage covenant, but let's make cultivating this union our lifelong quest.

> **❝** Covenant begins with a commitment, it is sustained by discipline, and it is evaluated by its productivity in making both people into someone better than they were when they began. **❞**

Covenant is an active relationship, not a static agreement. When Ruth chose to remain with her mother-in-law Naomi, she knew what was involved. Her decision committed her to a lifestyle of giving, serving, protecting, and being available. But for her, personal sacrifice was far more bearable than the pain of being separated from the person she loved.

For Further Study:
Need any motivation to get rid of pride? Here are just a few of God's promises to those who are humble: Ps 25:9, Pr 3:34, Isa 66:2, and 1Pe 5:6.

Covenant requires the grace of God. If we're not crying out for his grace, it's probably not so much laziness as it is pride—independent, self-reliant pride. And if we're proud we're in trouble, because God promises to resist us (1Pe 5:5). The worst thing we can do is think we've mastered the art of marriage. On the other hand, we experience God's grace when we admit our need for help. Whether we acknowledge it or not, each of us is in desperate need of God's wisdom, his creativity, and the fruit and gifts of the Spirit. Apart from a humble dependence on God, we'll never be able to fulfill our marriage covenant.

One final note on covenant. As you've probably guessed by now, a successful marriage is going to require patience and hard work. Are we willing to make the investment? Despite all this emphasis on sacrifice and death, marriage surpasses all other earthly treasures. No matter how much effort it requires, your marriage is worth far more than you'll ever put into it!

Leaving and Cleaving

As we've already seen, marriage is ordained and sustained by God. Without his grace, the responsibilities would make us throw up our hands and quit! But from the very beginning God made it clear that we play an active role in this, too: "For this cause a man shall leave his father and his mother, and shall cleave to his wife; and they shall become one flesh" (Ge 2:24 NAS). Underline the three verbs in that verse—leave, cleave, and become—and you'll have your marital job description. Let's see just what each of those involves.

Leaving. A wedding marks a point of departure. The bride and groom say goodbye to their former way of life and begin something new. Authority and loyalties change hands. New priorities must be established. Though still commanded to honor their parents, the couple makes a psychological, governmental, and usually a geographical shift away from the family of their childhood to their own new family.

For many spouses, especially those who grew up in loving families, leaving can be very difficult. Yet the marriage will never be healthy until you make the break. Wives, the verse quoted above doesn't specifically command you to leave your parents, but don't use that as a loophole. The union between husband and wife must have no rivals. That bond of mutual dependence is vital to the success of any marriage. Every couple should take pains to carefully define their own distinct, marital identity.

Leaving can also be a difficult adjustment for the parents, and we've observed that it is often the husband's mother who struggles most. As she watches another woman take first place in her son's life, the mother experiences the truth of the old proverb: "A daughter is a daughter all her life, a son is a son till he meets his wife." She may be affected deeply by the change.

Though parents do need to release their children, the couple can show honor by being patient and understanding through the adjustment period. It might even be helpful to sit down with your parents to thank them for their care and their help in preparing you to start a life of your own. Go on to express your awareness that the adjustment to your new priorities may be a challenge for them as well as you and ask for their understanding as you try to establish your new family identity and priorities. This one conversation, though awkward, could save you years of confusion and conflict.

---

5 Would any of the following statements make you nervous about your spouse's willingness to leave childhood behind?

❑ Husband: "Honey, could you call UPS? I've got a box of laundry I need to send out to Mom."

❑ Wife: "Sweetheart, you know that date you have planned? Well, I mentioned it to Dad...he's not sure I'm old enough for that."

❑ Husband: "Sugar, have you given me my weekly allowance yet?"

❑ Wife: "Great news, dear! My folks are coming to celebrate our anniversary with us!"

Cleaving. In the Hebrew (translated *dabaq*) this word has two definitions. It first means to cling, adhere, or stick. Often this is where couples stop in their marriage. Joined together by a formal agreement, they mistakenly think that's all it takes. But there's a second aspect of the word which means to catch by pursuit, to follow after, to keep fast, overtake, or pursue. The fact that we wooed and won our spouse doesn't mean the wooing and winning is over. A husband should continually be winning his wife's heart and affections. A wife should always be looking for fresh new ways to demonstrate her love for her husband. An "I do" and a marriage license on your wedding day won't suffice. Make cleaving an active and ongoing part of your marriage. A lasting relationship involves not only "I do" but "I will."

Becoming. Marriage is both instantaneous and ongoing. At the moment we enter into covenant with our spouse, two persons are united as one. And yet we continue to cultivate that union. Becoming one flesh requires active participation, not passive acceptance. It embraces every area of our being: spiritual, intellectual, emotional, and physical. Over time we should see our oneness constantly developing and deepening. This is what makes marriage a lifelong adventure!

The Power of Love

Having defined marriage and explored the significance of covenant, let's get really basic. What is love? What is this passionate force between husband and wife that makes a marriage work?

There's no way we can improve on the definition Scripture gives in 1 Corinthians, chapter 13. Paul's classic description of love is one of the most beautiful passages in the New Testament. The following points are simply intended to extract the principles from that chapter and show how they can be applied.

Love is the willing and consistent practice of laying down (sacrificing) one's life in order to meet the needs of another (1Jn 3:16-18). Because this kind of behavior is totally at odds with our selfish disposition, we don't assume every reader will accept this at face value. So let's ask the question: Why should we risk personal sacrifice to make a marriage work? At what point does sacrifice prove too costly?

Meditate on Matthew 19:4-6. Do you think today's divorce rate would drop if people understood God's role in and concern for marriage?

Marriage is a gift from God and is worth the highest possible investment. God's greatest gift, of course, is the relationship we enjoy with him, thanks to the substitutionary death of Jesus Christ on the cross. And our union with Christ enables us to experience something supernatural in our marriages. By his example, Jesus demonstrated that no sacrifice is too great for love.

Laying down your life doesn't mean you become your spouse's personal doormat. Love is not an open invitation to abuse. It won't force you to compromise your identity or safety. Sacrificial love simply means that when we reach the point of conflict, we consciously set aside our own selfish objectives and choose that which best serves God and our spouse. For example, suppose that I (Gary) come home from work, greet Betsy and the children, then sit down to read the newspaper. Betsy mentions that she would like to go for a walk with the children. No problem —until I realize she would like me to come along. On a good day I'll think to myself, *Reading this paper doesn't benefit our relationship. It benefits me. For the sake of our relationship and children, I'll go for a walk.* On a bad day...well, let's not talk about the bad days.

Being willing to lay down your life for your spouse may require that you risk conflict. At times a husband needs to lead his wife into agreement with a decision she doesn't like because he knows she will ultimately benefit. For the good of the marriage, love must sometimes take an unpopular stand.

Much of the material you are reading began as a seminar that Betsy and I teach at our church. The day I first came home from a pastors' meeting and announced we might be teaching this seminar, Betsy's first response was definitely not, "Oh! Could we?!?" It was more like, "What do you mean, 'We'?" Citing this as an opportunity to serve together, to overcome fear, and to develop her very evident gift for teaching, I was able to lead her into teaching the class and also into greater confidence and fruitfulness. (Then there was the time I came home to say, "Dear, did I tell you they want us to use our seminar notes...to write a *book?!*")

Love is an unconditional commitment to an imperfect person (Eph 2:4-5). God's love for us is illustration enough.

Love is not an emotion, but rather a decision (followed by action) to seek the good of another (Jn 3:16). Emotions had nothing to do with our Lord's choice to die on the cross. He knew the price of our redemption, and he made the painful decision to pay it. Though often supplemented by warm, pleasant feelings, love does not depend on them to do what is right. It's a decision we must make daily!

Love is unaffected by the attitude, activity, initiative, or responsiveness of your partner (Ro 5:8). Contrary to prevailing opinion, marriage is not a 50/50 partnership. Scripture commands us to give 100 percent regardless of, or even despite, our spouse's contribution! As a seminar speaker once said, "You can be the best husband in the world, and there's nothing your wife can do about it."

Think about that. This approach is totally unnatural, but here lies the secret of a successful marriage. If we love in order to be loved, we're setting ourselves up with expectations which can lead to disappointment, bitterness, resentment, and possibly to divorce. On the other hand, if we love in order to obey and honor God, recognizing him as Lord of our expectations, we can be fulfilled

> 66 Occasionally the immature bliss of honeymoon love yields to a growing relationship between people who notice their own flaws more than those of their mates, who are troubled more by their own selfishness than by that of their spouse, and who make it a priority to become better companions. These become the truly great marriages, and they are rare.[6] 99
> —**Larry Crabb**

For Further Study:
Read John 15:13. How did Jesus demonstrate this principle in his relationship with his disciples? with you?

whether our spouse reciprocates our love or not, because our ultimate satisfaction comes from pleasing God. Can you honestly make that declaration? We need God's Word to renew our minds to this ultimate purpose. When both husband and wife are walking in a close relationship with Jesus Christ and both are committed to giving their all, the benefits will be unimaginable.

Love is supernatural and must find its origin, its example, and its sustaining power in God (1Jn 4:16). Our ability to love hinges on our receiving, by faith, the love and acceptance of God. As John so succinctly expressed it, "We love because he first loved us" (1Jn 4:19). The kind of love God calls us to demonstrate to one another is exemplified in Jesus. It won't come naturally or effortlessly. We need to pray regularly for the power to love our spouse and build our marriage.

Love is a commandment (Jn 13:34). If for no other reason, love your spouse because God said to do it. Share this principle with unsaved friends or neighbors, though, and they'll probably question your sanity. Apart from salvation no one would or could live this way.

Love is a divine mandate to husbands and the responsibility of wives (Eph 5:25, Tit 2:4). Again, we must remember that the commandment to love as husband and wife is simply a more specialized application of our call to love one another because we are disciples of Jesus Christ (Jn 13:35). Love in marriage should produce an intimacy with one another which in essence reflects an intimacy with him.

Love is first and foremost our response to God, followed and demonstrated by a love for others (Mt 22:37-40). Again, John the apostle summed it up perfectly: "Whoever loves God must also love his brother" (1Jn 4:21). A true love for God will stir up our love for our spouse. And remember: Love said but not done isn't love.

---

6 How can you demonstrate your love for your spouse between now and the time you go to sleep tonight?

Here's Where Marriage Begins

Meditate on Amos 3:3. Do you and your spouse agree that God and his Word provide the only solid foundation for your marriage?

If you don't remember anything else you read in this book, please remember this: A magnificent marriage begins not with knowing one another but with knowing God. In him we have the foundation and resources necessary to love one another. His Word, his ways, and his will must be paramount in our lives. Unless we are growing in the knowledge of God, we'll lack the motivation and wisdom to build an effective marriage.

Knowing God gives us the creativity to be romantic; it gives us the grace to lead and follow. Faith toward God sustains, instructs, and motivates us. It's because we are seeking first the Lord and his kingdom that all things—including the tools for a magnificent marriage—shall be added to us.

If you have encountered trials and difficulties in your marriage, or if your marriage has not yet begun, give yourselves plenty of time to grow into the truths and principles we've covered in this first study. There's enough here to keep you busy for the rest of your married life! God doesn't expect you to attain perfection in the next 24 hours—or the next 24 years, for that matter, but he does expect faith and obedience. We advise you to start slowly, establish convictions, and concentrate on becoming consistent.

> ❝ The family belongs to God. He created it. He determined its inner structure. He appointed for it its purpose and goal. By divine permission, a man and a woman may cooperate with God's purpose and become a part of it. But the home they establish remains his establishment. 'Unless the Lord builds the house, those who build it labor in vain.'(Ps 127:1)...
>
> This is not our marriage, but his marriage; not our home, but his home; not our children, but his children; not our family, but his family. This might sound like pious rhetoric, but it works itself out in thoroughly down-to-earth fashion. If Jesus is truly Lord in your family, it will influence everything from the way you decorate your home to the way you spend your summer vacation.[7] ❞
>
> —**Larry Christenson**

Ladies, if your husbands begin to demonstrate love after a long season of neglect, be patient and receive their love thankfully. Please don't say, "Well, you're only doing that because it said to in the book. You don't really mean it." It may feel that way for awhile, but they need to start somewhere.

The first steps to marital restoration may be very awkward. It's difficult to admit, "You know, I've never said this to you before, but in my heart this is what I want our relationship to be like. I haven't done a good job at it, but

I want to. I don't know how, but be patient with me as I try." It's the first step that's the hardest, but God will honor every effort we make to change. ◼

GROUP DISCUSSION

▶ Briefly describe your parents' relationship. Has their example affected your view of marriage?

▶ On page 6 the authors say, "Significance is found in giving your life away, not in selfishly trying to find personal happiness." Ladies, if *Ms.* magazine asked you to respond to that statement, what would you say?

▶ What are some ways (private and public) to honor your spouse?

▶ How can you demonstrate that you take your marriage covenant as seriously as God does?

▶ What has it been like for you to break from your parents and start a new life with your spouse?

▶ What do you want your spouse to experience in marriage?

▶ Do you consider divorce an option for Christians? Why or why not?

▶ Why is a growing relationship with God critical to a growing relationship with your spouse?

▶ Is there any danger in having high expectations for your marriage?

▶ Take a few minutes to pray for one another as couples. Ask God to deepen and strengthen your marriages as you work through this book.

RECOMMENDED READING

Strengthening Your Marriage by Wayne Mack (Phillipsburg, NJ: Presbyterian and Reformed Publishing Company, © 1977)

DROP THAT FIG LEAF!

GARY AND BETSY RICUCCI

SCRIPTURE TEXT   Genesis 2:25

WARM-UP   What percentage of American couples refuse to take a bath or shower together?

A. 7%

B. 21%

C. 37%

D. 54%

E. 69%

(See page 33 for answer)

PERSONAL STUDY   Maybe you've experienced something similar...Betsy and I had spent the evening with friends in our home, and were cleaning up the kitchen before going to bed. Had you watched us working together you would have thought we were the model of marital harmony...until I realized I could still catch the sports on the ten o'clock news and slipped downstairs to watch it.

When I came back upstairs the house was clean. The crumbs were swept up and the dishes were all put away. Betsy was quiet. At first I thought, *Well, she's had a long day. She probably doesn't have much to talk about.* But it didn't take long to realize this silence wasn't caused by fatigue. She was upset. Rather than launching into a tirade about how I had left her to do all the work, she continued her bedtime preparations in deafening silence. (Quite a testimony to her self-control, considering all she *could* have said.)

At moments like this, it's easy for men to assume things are fine. They may even prefer the quiet. But things are not fine. In marriage, no news is *not* good news. And at these times, silence between husband and wife is very unhealthy.

Our need to communicate dates back to creation. When God saw that Adam lacked a suitable companion, he declared, "It is not good for the man to be alone." This was not a conclusion Adam reached on his own; at least not yet. God had to tell Adam, just like he needs to regularly remind us. It's not good to be alone. The apparent peace of independence and isolation is a delusion at best, and destructive at worst. Men, in God's economy we are incomplete without our wives!

Now he could have scooped up a fresh handful of dust and made Eve from scratch—a totally independent creature—but he didn't. He chose to form her from the man, from one of Adam's ribs (Ge 2:18-23). As a result, married men and women have an inherent, God-given need and desire to fit back into one another's lives. That's the essence of communication.

Yet just because it's God-given doesn't mean it's easy. If a couple fails to walk in the light of honest communication, their marriage could be described as two people stumbling around in a dark room. Inevitably one bumps into the other and someone gets hurt. Because neither saw or understood what happened, the explanations and interpretations can vary widely.

"Hey—you hurt me!"

"What do you mean? You hurt *me!*"

"Look, it was an accident."

"Was not. You did it on purpose."

> **❝** When we regard our wrong actions as understandable, we feel only a little guilty. Movement from self-centeredness... happens only when we expose our excuses for selfishness and regard those excuses as entirely illegitimate.[1] **❞**
>
> —**Larry Crabb**

Not only is the room dark, but it's cluttered with numerous obstacles—immaturity, bad experiences in other relationships, or cultural trends that weaken our commitment to marriage. Fortunately, as John's first letter explains, "God is light...If we walk in the light, as he is in the light, we have fellowship with one another, and the blood of Jesus, his Son, purifies us from all sin" (1Jn 1:5,7).

Making excuses or blaming others for our own disobedience is never acceptable. Regardless of our experience and subsequent sinful attitudes, behavior, or patterns of speech, God has given us power through his Spirit and Word to forgive, to repent, and to be transformed.

1 As we grow up, our personalities are influenced by other people, events, and circumstances—an absentee dad, perhaps, or a series of moves from city to city. In the space below, list two or three of the primary influences that contributed to making you who you are today.

-

-

-

Communication is risky. It means being open—emotionally naked, if you will. It requires a commitment to reveal yourself, even when there are certain things you'd rather hide. Communicating simply means exposing who you are: what you like and don't like; what you regret or look forward to; where you're confident and where you're afraid.

We have to be careful, though, that our communication doesn't become selfish. As a homemaker with young children, I (Betsy) have a desire to be understood which tends to peak around 5:00 or 5:30 in the afternoon...just as Gary is walking in the door. All the difficulties of my day—the red paint spilled on the carpet, the numerous quarrels I've refereed—are right on my lips, ready to spill out. Yet no matter how much I may want to vent, my responsibility is not to be understood but to understand. How was *his* day? What pressures has *he* encountered?

Meditate on Philippians 2:3-4.
What is one thing you could do today for your spouse to apply these verses?

It takes a lot of self-discipline to focus on him, and I don't always succeed. Sometimes if he's recounting the rough spots of his day I feel like saying, "Well, my day hasn't been any picnic either, fella." But godly communication concerns itself first with knowing rather than being known. As we strive to meet our spouse's needs, God will make sure our own needs are met.

Learning to Listen

Imagine yourself during the Alaskan gold rush, pick in hand, staring at a huge gold nugget you've just unearthed from your mine. Would you stop there? Would you take

23

the next train home, musing to yourself, "Well that was profitable. I found a nugget of gold"? Of course not! You would dig more than ever. If necessary you would work night and day until you had extracted every ounce of the precious metal from that vein.

> **"** True success is never an easy achievement. Happy and fulfilling marriages are products of extreme effort. They are desired, sought after, fought for, and planned. They never just happen.[2] **"**
>
> **—Donald R. Harvey**

Whether you recognize it or not, your marriage is a gold mine full of priceless treasure waiting to be discovered. Communication serves as your pick. As you pursue your spouse and persevere in your quest to understand him or her, you'll find marriage is a fascinating and rewarding adventure.

Going after your mate with a pick may seem a bit indelicate, so here's another illustration: "The purposes of a man's heart are deep waters, but a man of understanding draws them out" (Pr 20:5). Throughout our married life we should regularly be lowering the bucket into the well of our spouse's heart and pulling up new feelings, desires, and interests. Newlyweds will probably find more surprises per bucket, but deep communication is an adventure for not-so-newlyweds as well. Your spouse is marvelously complex. The well will never run dry, no matter how long you're married.

---

2 During a routine conversation with your spouse you learn the following information. Which of these revelations would surprise you most?

❏ Your spouse is a direct descendant of King Louis XIV

❏ Your spouse grew up on a farm with six brothers and five sisters

❏ Your spouse has false teeth

❏ Your spouse has no idea where babies come from

❏ Your spouse has a secret fear of talking in public

❏ Your spouse is wanted in 17 states for armed robbery

Though Betsy and I have been married over 15 years, there are plenty of times when I don't understand what she's feeling. That's okay. Neither of us expects the other to read our mind (most of the time!). What's crucial, though, is that I show Betsy my *desire* to understand her. She won't be offended if I have difficulty relating to her feelings, as long as she sees I'm making an attempt. By telling Betsy I want to understand, I free her from the pressure of having to rationally explain every remark— especially if her statements are confrontational. But if I sit there with a blank or annoyed expression on my face, we're going to have a problem.

The way you listen to your spouse can either make or break your communication. If you're a good listener, you'll give your undivided attention. That means turning off the TV, tuning out other conversations, and putting down the newspaper. If you're at a restaurant, it means picking a seat where you won't be distracted by other people. But keep your expectations within reason. If I begin talking to Betsy while she is making dinner for guests due to arrive at any minute, I don't expect her to shut off the stove, sit down at the table, and hang on my every word. I simply want the benefit of her thoughts and feelings, even if those are occasionally interrupted by the baby, the blender, or the microwave.

Meditate on Proverbs 10:19 and 18:13. According to these verses, would you characterize your communication as wisdom or folly?

Maintain good eye contact when listening to your spouse. Look at one another! Some may find this awkward at first, but it's a habit worth cultivating. There is no one we should be more secure with or more respectful toward than the person we married. You could take an evening out together just to discuss the extent to which this is your experience.

Another basic tip that can do wonders for communication: simply nod your head, or use a similar form of body language. This signals that you're interested and comprehend what is being said. It's no fun speaking to someone who is stone-faced. On the other hand, your spouse may question your sincerity if you bob your head like one of those maddening toy dogs with its head on a spring, mocking you from the rear window of a car that's going 15 mph under the speed limit. A periodic nod, facial expression, or gentle touch can show you are hearing, participating, and understanding.

Though structurally identical, a husband's ears and wife's ears seem to function quite differently. For example, men tend to hear what their wives say, analyze it, then quickly draw a conclusion or propose a strategy. While this comes as second-nature for many men, it can be arrogant and condescending. "He who answers before listening—that is his folly and his shame," said Solomon

25

For Further Study:
How did Job respond
when God confronted
him for speaking too
quickly? (See Job 40:
1-5)

(Pr 18:13). It may also be a not-so-subtle way of saying, "I want to get this out of the way so I can get on with what's really important" or "The solution is so obvious, I can't believe you had to ask!" If you want to turn a three-minute conversation into a three-hour conflict, respond to your wife's next problem by saying, "Well, what you should have done is..."

Instead of giving short, terse answers, train yourself to listen patiently to your spouse. This one discipline could prevent the overwhelming majority of your conflicts from ever occurring. Don't assume you know all the factors involved—ask questions. Probe beneath the surface. Your understanding will probably be a far greater asset to her than your "solutions." Besides, our wives already know most of the answers; they just need to know we identify with them.

cathy®   by **Cathy Guisewite**

Women are typically more concerned than men about the details of communication. Someone has said men are the headlines, while women are the fine print. This is definitely true in our marriage. When I (Gary) hear someone has had a new baby, I ask two questions: Boy or girl? Is everyone healthy? That satisfies my curiosity. But when I share the news with Betsy, it's like starting a computer program! What's the baby's name? (Same as the parents'.) Weight and length? (I didn't think to ask.) How long was she in transition? (From where to where?) How long was the labor? (Long enough to get the job done.) We've laughed about this fundamental difference in our communication since we were married, and this particular illustration is still fresh today!

Wives, do your best to trust your husband's motives in this area. He's not trying to be insensitive. He just happens to be satisfied with the headlines—a trait, by the way, that perfectly complements your emphasis on detail.

Years ago I heard a man share the following homespun wisdom about the way women are made: "Not that you'll understand *why* she's thata' way, but you can just understand that she *is* thata' way. And God made her thata' way, and you can fast and pray till you don't weigh ten pounds and she'll still be thata' way!" Trying to make your spouse exactly like yourself is as futile and foolish as trying to make water run uphill. You are different by design. God fashioned you to complement one another, and a complement is defined as "that which is required to supply a deficiency" or "the necessary opposite part." Complementary colors are on opposite ends of the color wheel. Our different approaches to life will undoubtedly generate some tension, but those differences are both necessary and healthy.

Accept your spouse the way he or she is, then use those distinctions to enhance your life and marriage. By working together as a team, appreciating each other's perspectives, you will gain a clearer understanding of life's issues and problems. If that's not enough motivation, think of it this way: If you were both the same, one of you wouldn't be necessary.

---

3 One night you discover a surprise message from your best friends on the answering machine: "Guess what? We're moving to Botswana this weekend! Hope to see you before we go. Bye!"

You immediately pick up the phone and call. What are the first three questions you will ask them?

-

-

-

(Compare notes with your spouse. How did your questions differ?)

A marriage commonly features one spouse who gravitates toward objective facts and observations (often the husband) and one who specializes in feelings and discernment. Those personality traits lead to different styles of communication. The spouse who deals with information only says things once. The spouse who deals with intuition may repeat a comment many times, each with a different shade of meaning. That can frustrate the one who wants, "Just the facts, ma'am."

I've learned that the first time I hear Betsy say something, I get the information. The second time will tell me the issue is important. The third time tells me whether she feels good or bad about the issue. I may even hear it a fourth time, which may well signal her concern over my lack of concern about the matter! Repetition is an important part of her communication. It's her way of expressing emotions. And even if the words are the same, each repetition communicates something new. It's my job to interpret what Betsy is feeling as well as thinking. I've got to keep lowering my bucket until I find what's in her heart.

A healthy marriage will leave plenty of opportunity for expressing emotions. However, unchecked emotions quickly lead to a downward and destructive spiral. At times I (Betsy) have needed Gary to stop me in my emotional tracks and warn me about the consequences of prolonged discouragement,

---

TEN COMMANDMENTS FOR BETTER COMMUNICATION

■ Learn to express your feelings and frustrations honestly, but without accusing or attacking the other person (Pr 11:9).

■ Choose words, expressions, and a tone of voice that are kind and gentle. Don't use speech that could easily offend or spark an argument (Pr 15:1).

■ Do not exaggerate, distort, or stretch the truth. Avoid extreme words like "never" and "always" (Eph 4:25).

■ Give actual and specific examples—if necessary, make notes before you communicate. Stay away from generalities.

■ Commit yourself to seeking solutions rather than merely airing your grievances. Getting even isn't the goal—you want to get things resolved (Ro 12:17-21).

■ Listen to what the other person is saying, feeling, and needing. Try to detect his or her underlying concerns (Jas 1:19).

■ Refuse to indulge bitterness, anger, withdrawal, or argument. Though these emotions are normal, indulging them is sin (Eph 4:26).

■ Be quick to acknowledge your own failure, and don't hesitate to forgive the other person. Make sure you don't still hold a grudge (Lk 17:3-4).

■ Keep talking and asking questions until you are sure you both understand clearly what the other is saying and feeling. Encourage each other as you press toward a solution (Ro 14:19).

■ Train your mouth and heart until you can say the right thing at the right time in the right way for the right reasons!

unbelief, or fear. Sometimes I've responded, "But this is how I feel! You don't understand!" Yet ladies, it is possible for a husband to give too much understanding and too little direction. Our emotions should never be the final authority on what is reality and what isn't. They shouldn't dominate our life or mandate our responses or behavior. Sometimes what I need most is to repent—not vent. A timely word from your husband may be God's means of saving you from an emotional "crash and burn."

That's not a role I (Gary) enjoy. Knowing when to console and when to counsel takes the grace of God. Speak out one second too soon and your good intentions may go up in smoke. So much of communication is a hair's breadth away from a conflict! Expect to learn through trial and error. And though you may be uncertain about the timing, at least make sure your motive is right. If you're trying to do anything other than help your spouse, swallow your comments (and your pride) and wait.

Hide and Seek

Before they sinned, Adam and Eve were naked and unashamed (Ge 2:25). They had nothing to hide, and were completely open and intimate. But look what happened as soon as they ate the forbidden fruit: "Then the eyes of both of them were opened, and they realized they were naked; so they sewed fig leaves together and made coverings for themselves" (Ge 3:7).

Their new wardrobe represents much more than a sudden concern for modesty. Sin made Adam and Eve acutely (and proudly) self-conscious, and their first thought was to hide—not just from God, but from each other. This degenerated into guilt, blame-shifting, and no doubt resentment and bitterness as well. The same can happen to us. If we don't go to the cross of Jesus Christ with our pride and selfishness, it's going to be Adam and Eve all over again!

During the centuries since, man has perfected the art of hiding. We conceal everything from pimples to our past. As we start our relationship we work hard to look and act our best. What are we doing? Hiding! Then we get married and there's no longer a place to hide.

Perhaps you're embarrassed about your weight or some physical blemish and try to cover it up. Maybe you seek to avoid situations that could be painful or awkward, or you've got a problem with another person that you

For Further Study: Is there anything Corinthian about your relationship with your spouse? (See 2Co 6:11-13)

don't know how to solve. Rather than ask for advice from your spouse you plow ahead and become increasingly defensive. These walls may be small to begin with, but if you develop a habit of hiding from your spouse, they grow thicker and higher. It's possible for a couple to cut off all contact with each other, to become strangers under the same roof.

Our sinfulness will tempt us to hide, withdraw, and avoid. And yet God commands us to demonstrate transparency, honesty, and vulnerability. Those traits are possible only because of the work Christ has done within us—a work of transforming grace which should affect all of our relationships, particularly marriage.

Men, your wife wants to know more than your bowling average and the make of your favorite car. Ladies, your husband wants to know more than your fudge recipe and favorite classical composer. Genuine understanding requires that we reveal our fears, ambitions, desires, thoughts, dreams, convictions, reactions, failures, and faults. The more fully we know and are known, the more security and intimacy we will enjoy in marriage.

One caution: self-expression shouldn't overrule self-control. It is possible to say things that are painfully honest without devastating your spouse in the process. Note that the Proverbs 31 woman "speaks with wisdom, and faithful instruction is on her tongue" (Pr 31:26).

---

4 Which of the questions below, if asked by your spouse, might tempt you to hide or be evasive?

❏ "Are you satisfied with your relationship with God?"

❏ "If you could change one thing about me, what would it be?"

❏ "What is your biggest fear in life?"

❏ "Are you happy with the state of our marriage?"

❏ "How could I serve you better in our physical intimacy?"

❏ "Why did you marry me?"

Because we know ourselves so well, we commonly assume our spouses know exactly what we are thinking or feeling at any given moment. *Doesn't he know I'm too frazzled to think about sex? Can't she see how much I need some time alone?* It seems so obvious. But mind-reading shouldn't be a requirement for marriage. Why do you think God created speech? Unless we tell our spouses what we think and feel, they won't be able to help us. Our expectations will lead to frustration and eventually to conflict. By that point we've typically pre-judged the other, and things go from bad to worse. With a little humility and communication up front, though, the whole cycle could be avoided.

> **❝** Even though our natural tendency is to cover ourselves, I believe that in marriage God still allows us to reveal ourselves with a safety that no other relationship can give. In the sanctity of marriage, we can drop our guard and show ourselves to our partners. This does not come automatically, but with effort and acceptance from your partner, it pays huge dividends.[3] **❞**
>
> —**Conrad Smith**

It can be hard to tell your spouse about something you need or want. It seems selfish. Yet that interchange is crucial if we want to fulfill our roles in marriage. Eve was created to be Adam's helper (Ge 2:20). If a husband won't let his wife into his life, her ability to help is severely limited. Similarly, if the wife doesn't open up to her husband, he will lack the input he needs to serve effectively as her spiritual head.

This may sound mystical, but ask God to open your heart to your spouse, to help you feel what he or she feels. I (Gary) remember an outreach years ago when Betsy and I witnessed to a group of teenagers at the local mall. They weren't very interested. When Betsy tried sharing, they laughed. She was in tears when we got home.

At the time I thought, *Don't take it so hard—teenagers do that sort of thing.* I doubt I was much comfort. But weeks later I was sitting in my office and began thinking about the experience. Suddenly I was affected emotionally. I began feeling what Betsy must have felt. My eyes filled with tears as I realized how embarrassing it must have been for her, how painful. She stepped out in faith and all she got was ridicule and rejection. God had opened my heart. I'm not sure I could handle such intense emotions daily, but this revelation gave me a greater desire to know what's going on in Betsy's heart so I can better lead, support, and encourage her.

One final point about openness and honesty. Men frequently suppress their emotions without even knowing it. We had been married six years before I (Betsy) discovered Gary didn't really know himself emotionally. For example, I would hear him describe a situation in which he had

For Further Study:
Sometimes it *can* be selfish to tell your spouse your desires, as whining King Ahab demonstrates in 1 Kings 21:1-16.

been wronged, and I'd ask, "Are you angry? Did that hurt you?" He would shrug it off as if it hadn't affected him. But as I persistently lowered my bucket and kept asking questions, he began to acknowledge that maybe he did feel a bit hurt. It's not that he was trying to be evasive. He simply didn't understand how he felt. Often he's aware that his feelings are a secondary issue in obedience and decision-making, and so he doesn't share them. But as I continue drawing him out, he's learning that it's important for me to know how he feels.

I became somewhat of a detective, searching Gary for clues that would reveal what was going on inside him. Soon I could detect a great deal by the way his jaw was set; the way he came up the sidewalk; the way he would shut the front door or greet the children. I've found that an afternoon phone call helps me find out how he is doing so I know what to expect when he comes home. That way I'm predisposed to understand and adapt to his situation rather than dump my agenda on him. Also, by keeping track of his responsibilities and appointments I'm able to anticipate his needs and look for creative ways to serve him.

> " In a dialogue, neither person is required to give up, to quit, or to give in—only to give of him or herself. In a dialogue we never end up with less, but only more. Joys are doubled by exchange, and burdens are cut in half by sharing.[4] "
>
> —Ed Wheat

Men, it would be well worth your while to consider the things that routinely affect your wife's emotions, and thus her communication. Was she awake with a sick child during the night? Where is she in her menstrual cycle? (This affects more than just verbal communication!) Was she able to do all she had hoped to get done during the day? A quick call from work could make the difference between the spaghetti hitting your plate or hitting the fan!

Our marital relationship will only progress as far as our ability to communicate. You may find it easier to hide behind a fig leaf rather than reveal yourself to your mate. That's a safe place, but it's a lonely place. And isolation doesn't really stay safe for long; eventually God reveals your pride and flushes you out.

In addition to being open, humble, and intimate with your spouse you need to be vulnerable with others in your church. Every couple needs at least one other couple who knows and loves them enough to ask the hard questions:

"What prompted that comment you made about your finances last Friday?"

"With all the demands of the new job, are you spending enough time with your wife?"

"When did you last go out on a date together?"

"You haven't seemed yourself recently—what's wrong?"

"How are you pursuing your children's spiritual development?"

Don't wait for them to ask questions or volunteer their comments—ask them. Beg them! Their timely insights could spare you and your spouse a lot of frustration.

Honest communication is at times awkward, painful, and risky. It takes courage to be vulnerable. But if you hope to experience God's will for your marriage—the partnership, fellowship, and intimacy he intended from the beginning—you'll stop hiding and start talking. ■

GROUP DISCUSSION

❱ What is the silliest argument you and your spouse have ever had?

❱ On page 23, the authors describe communication as being "emotionally naked." What does that mean to you?

❱ Describe a situation where you were pleasantly surprised to discover something new about your spouse.

Answer to Warm-Up
(from page 21): C. 37%
(Source: *What Counts: The Complete Harper's Index*, p.172)

❱ What attitudes or actions make a marriage boring?

❱ In what areas of communication do you excel? (Men, I suggest you let your wife answer for you first!)

❱ In what areas could you use some help?

❱ "Security in marriage is a function of transparency." Is this true? Why or why not?

❱ Did you learn anything new about listening in this study?

RECOMMENDED READING

The Drifting Marriage by Donald R. Harvey, Ph.D. (Old Tappan, NJ: Fleming H. Revell Company, © 1988)

The Intimate Marriage by R.C. Sproul (Wheaton, IL: Tyndale House Publishers, © 1990)

WHAT'S JAMMING THE SIGNALS?

GARY AND BETSY RICUCCI

SCRIPTURE TEXT Proverbs 16:23-24

WARM-UP On average, how much time is required to translate the Bible into a new language?

A. 1 year

B. 5 years

C. 10 years

D. 15 years

E. 20 years or more

(See page 48 for answer)

PERSONAL STUDY Communicating effectively involves transmitting information to another person in such a way that he or she can accurately receive it, clearly understand it, and properly respond to it. For example, suppose a businessman wants to contact potential customers in Burma and make them aware of a new product line. His objective is to get a detailed description of the goods into their hands by the end of the day. Where does he start?

As you know, just shouting toward Asia wouldn't do the job. Communication doesn't happen unless the information is *received*. So he decides to transmit his product announcement via fax machine. Yet he still has to send the message in a language the customers can *understand*. Otherwise his prized list will be curiously glanced at and discarded as gibberish. Finally, some explanation would have to be given so that his potential Burmese customers knew how to *respond*.

Communicating in marriage requires the same three essential ingredients: reception, understanding, and response. Assuming you and your spouse at least speak the same language and live on the same continent, we want to alert you to a number of other factors that can completely jam your communication signals. Have you had any experience with these?

Weak Transmitter. This particular technical difficulty is more common in the male species. Though structurally sound and properly equipped, he just won't communicate. Men, having been to the shop for repairs on several occasions myself, let me save you a lot of time diagnosing the problem...nine times out of ten it's laziness or selfishness. Here are the kinds of signals this equipment gives off: "Not now." "I'm too tired." "I've worked hard all day." (Be careful—that one in particular can generate a strong electrical surge from the receiver!) "Let's spend the evening watching a video together." "I don't have much to say."

At times this problem is difficult to diagnose because the reasons can sound legitimate. Besides, the husband in question is a good provider and he really *does* love his wife. But as necessary as these are, they are no substitute for communication. The responsibility for consistent, honest, and intimate conversation rests with the husband. He is to lead by his example and initiative, and he is to lead as a servant.

Obsolete Model. It's common to hear one spouse or the other explain a lack of communication like this: "That's not my personality." "Talking is not one of my strengths." "That's just the way I am."

Once again the problem is easily diagnosed. These are called *excuses*. And before we cling too tenaciously to the way we are by nature, we'd better remember that our old nature is precisely what sent Jesus to the cross! The Christian life should be a continual process of change and transformation. While giving each of us unique personalities, God does expect conformity to the image of his Son. That means serving, and in the context of marriage that means communicating. The model isn't obsolete. If we'll just

> " So-called emotional incompatibility is a myth invented by jurists short of arguments in order to plead for divorce. It is likewise a common excuse people use in order to hide their own failings. I simply do not believe it exists. There are no emotional incompatibilities. There are misunderstandings and mistakes, however, which can be corrected where there is the willingness to do so.[1] "
>
> —Paul Tournier

For Further Study:
Read Romans 12:2 and Ephesians 4:22-24. According to these verses, what process does conversion start in the life of a believer?

look in the manual, we'll find it's a lot more versatile than we thought.

When I (Gary) come home after a long day at work, it would be easier not to talk. It's an added expenditure of energy. Sometimes I feel too tired even to think. But those feelings are fundamentally lazy and selfish. If I'm going to love my wife, I've got to set aside my excuses and communicate.

---

1 Effective communication requires that we receive, understand, and respond. Can you identify which ingredient is missing in each of the statements below?

- "Yeah, I can see you're upset—so what do you want me to do about it?"

- Zzzzzzzzz. "Oh…must have dozed off. Sorry, honey—what was that you were saying?"

- "Wait a minute. You lost me. What do you mean, I don't listen well?"

Overly Specialized Equipment. Many men and women faithfully fulfill what they consider their essential duties in marriage: earning income, decorating the home, maintaining the yard, doing the shopping, and so on. The problem is, they leave communication off the list. They consider the function for which they have been programmed to be demanding enough, and trust that the communication program is in their spouse's software. "Look," says the stereotypical man, "I have worked all day. I have provided for my family. There is food on the table and a roof over our heads. Are you trying to tell me I've got to talk, too?" Sometimes it's the wife who can't understand the priority of meaningful conversation. But if a marriage is going to grow, both sides need to take responsibility for communicating.

Meditate on Hebrews 10:24-25. What two things does this passage command us to do for—and receive from—others?

At the same time, neither spouse should expect the other to meet all his or her needs for communication. That's why God created other members in the body of Christ. Interacting with friends provides valuable support for even the healthiest marriages. There have been times when I (Betsy) will call a girlfriend late in the afternoon and say, "You won't believe my day!" Then we'll start laughing as we compare the thrills and spills we've been through in the past eight hours. I often find that a short 10-minute call like this can help me welcome Gary with a receptive attitude when he comes home.

Men have the same need for relationships. They just don't think they do. When we have other couples in our home, the conversation often splits off in two different directions. The women immediately start talking about relationships, children, and things which affect them personally. Meanwhile the guys head out to the deck to discuss intensely emotional topics like our neighbor's immaculate lawn, pressure-treated lumber, or professional football. This group may have gotten together a dozen times before, but the men still talk about the same things. Embarrassing! Oddly enough, we go away feeling bonded together and relationally enriched. How's that for blissful ignorance?…and deception?!

Inter-fear-ence. Fear can short-circuit communication and leave nothing but silence. Some husbands and wives are so wary of rejection that they hesitate to share anything personal. They think to themselves, *What if she doesn't like this idea? What if he thinks my dreams for our future are foolish? How will this be perceived?* Some of these fears stem from past experiences—perhaps a parent or teacher who once said derisively, "That's the most ridiculous thing I've ever heard of." These things affect us. One of the best ways to deal with painful memories like this is to get them out on the table and begin talking. Fear must be faced and fought head-on.

Other communication glitches include the fear of burdening your spouse with your problems, or the fear of an argument if you discuss something confrontational. As far as the first is concerned, you shouldn't need any more encouragement to communicate than this advice from Solomon: "Two are better than one…If one falls down, his friend can help him up. But pity the man who falls and has no one to help him up!" (Ecc 4:9,10) Secondly, recognize that continual and consistent communication is your best strategy for minimizing conflict. The more frequently you talk with each other, the less you'll encounter smoldering resentments or major misunderstandings.

> 66 The "I cannot understand" really means "I cannot understand that my husband is different from me, that he thinks, feels, and acts in a quite different manner than I." So the husband feels judged, condemned, criticized. All of us fear this, for no one is satisfied with himself. We are especially sensitive to blame for shortcomings which we ourselves find stupid, and which we have never been able to correct in spite of our sincerest efforts.[2] 99
>
> —**Paul Tournier**

What distinguishes the
two types of people
described in Proverbs
9:8? Which category did
David fall in? (See Ps
141:5.) How about you?

High Voltage. Because we care for each other and want God's best for each other, loving correction should be a desired and active ingredient in every marriage. As the Lord sanctifies us he calls us to change and bear fruit in areas of attitude, character, and behavior. Often God uses the other spouse to spotlight the need for change, which means he or she must be willing to communicate.

For most of us, confrontation is an area of service we'd rather avoid. It's especially difficult when experience tells us our spouse will react defensively. If your husband or wife turns hostile or withdraws every time you raise a concern, you may be tempted to compromise honesty in the interest of maintaining peace. It will be hard to take that step of communication.

We'll take an in-depth look at conflict resolution in the next study, but here's one practical piece of advice: Regularly remind your spouse that you want him or her to adjust you, to help you become more like Jesus. Use the twenty questions on pages 44 and 45 to solicit correction. You'll need more than a little of God's grace to receive that adjustment when it comes, but at least your spouse will feel the freedom to approach you.

---

2 One author personifies wrong approaches to confrontation with the following fictitious characters. Do you resemble any of them?

❑ Henry the Hintdropper: "I can't believe it…Frank's wife puts romantic notes in his lunch bag two or three times a week!"

❑ Mary the Manipulator: "Carl, you should take night classes and improve yourself."

❑ Gary the Guilt-tripper: "Well, if *that's* all I mean to you…okay then…no problem from me."

❑ Ivan the Intimidator: "Do you realize how incredibly rude you were to me at dinner tonight?!"

❑ Sarah the Stonewaller: "No…nothing's wrong (sigh). I'll get over it (moan)."[3]

Static! When you perceive something deficient about your marriage or your spouse, what kind of language do you use to express that? Have you ever found yourself saying, "You left the windows down, again!…You always throw your clothes on the floor…Why don't you ever take me out for a date?"

Rather than hurling accusations at your spouse, ask questions. Find out what happened and why it happened before assuming the worst. Not only will your spouse respond more favorably, but nine times out of ten you'll discover that your assessment of the problem was incomplete. Also, steer clear of words like "always," "never," and other extremes. These are almost *always* inaccurate, and you'll get a lot more discussed without them.

Meditate on Proverbs 25:15. Remember this next time you get into conflict with your spouse.

Before you became a Christian, you may have spent years perfecting ungodly patterns of speech. "But now," writes Paul, "you must rid yourselves of all such things as these: anger, rage, malice, slander, and filthy language from your lips" (Col 3:8). He expands on this in his letter to the Ephesians: "Do not let any unwholesome talk come out of your mouths, but only what is helpful for building others up according to their needs, that it may benefit those who listen…Get rid of all bitterness, rage and anger, brawling and slander, along with every form of malice" (Eph 4:29,31).

FOUR FACTS ABOUT ANGER

■ Anger is not the problem or the main emotion. Anger is a symptom!

■ Expressing your anger to your partner does not lessen your anger. It usually increases it!

■ How you use your anger was learned. This means you can learn a new response and get it under control.

■ Your partner is not responsible for making you angry. You are![4]

—**H. Norman Wright**

Re-educating your heart and mind and taming your tongue will take time, effort, and perseverance. Some may face major habits of speech like rage or filthy language; others may find their communication tinged with frustration, harshness, or criticism. An important first step is to discern your own particular weaknesses. I (Betsy) know I have a tendency to finish Gary's sentences for him. He doesn't particularly appreciate that. I sometimes interrupt him when he's speaking. Often I jump to conclusions, or share how I would have handled a situation differently. None of these things benefits Gary, and I certainly wouldn't want him to communicate the same way with me. So I'm trying to tame my tongue.

As we've discussed, men must resist the urge to provide a quick answer. I (Gary) find it far too easy to say, "Oh, just do this" or "Well, then don't do that." In order to change I need to focus on understanding what happened, when it happened, why it happened, and how Betsy felt it happened. Only then am I ready to respond. But here's the incentive: Investing a little time to be patient and understanding will save you hours of conflict.

---

3 What is your biggest weakness in the area of communication?

What do you see as your spouse's primary weakness in communication?

By this point you're probably thinking to yourself, *Do they really expect me to follow "96 Steps Toward Perfect Communication" every time I open my mouth? I might as well take a vow of silence.* But overarching these guidelines for communication is our commitment to love and forbearance. Scripture teaches us to "Be kind and compassionate to one another, forgiving each other, just as in Christ God forgave you" (Eph 4:32).

Determine to communicate in a way that builds up rather than tearing down. When you fall short, though, receive forgiveness and press on. The process may seem long at first, but as your mind is renewed by the Word of God eventually your tongue will develop new habits.

Make Time To Take Time

A steady flow of communication is one of the best indicators of life in a marriage. Scheduling times for communication is essential, as we'll see in a few paragraphs, but spontaneous conversation is equally important. How do you relate with each other throughout the day? A casual conversation over breakfast, a call at work, a scribbled note on a napkin—these keep the relationship fresh and growing. It doesn't take three hours of one-on-one discussion to say, "I'm interested in you. I value your companionship. Did you know you're my best friend?"

For Further Study:
When we obey the
instruction given in 1
Thessalonians 5:11,
who are we imitating?
(See Ro 15:5.)

Look specifically for ways to encourage your spouse,
then spread that throughout the day. Compliment her on
how she looks. Congratulate him on a job well done at
work. You'll be amazed at the way communication thrives
in an atmosphere of mutual encouragement and gratitude.

Someone has suggested that the way you greet each
other at day's end can determine the mood in your home
for the whole evening. Now a cloudy greeting doesn't have
to mean a stormy evening. But this is a wonderful window
of opportunity. Anticipate that moment when you're back
under the same roof, and use it as a chance to communicate your pleasure at being together with the one you
love. Husbands, if your wife has spent the day caring for
young children, she will probably be eager for some adult
conversation. Lay down your life—and your newspaper—
and give her your ears...both of them.

When your spouse calls you at work, view it as an
unexpected delight—not an interruption. Nothing on
your agenda for that day takes higher priority than communicating with your wife or husband. This doesn't mean
you must have a lengthy conversation; if you are in the
middle of a meeting, it's appropriate to say so. But your
spouse instinctively knows the difference between your
not having time to talk and your viewing the call as an
interruption. Never, never, never give the signal that his
or her call is a bother. And by the way: if it's clear that
your spouse is calling with a significant need, interrupt
your meeting—no matter how important—and take the
time to listen.

---

4 Looking back over the past 24 hours, list every time
slot—no matter how brief—in which you communicated with your spouse.

Is this a normal amount of communication for you? Does
it seem like a healthy amount?

**Meditate on
Ephesians 5:15-16.**
Are you making the
most of the time God
has given you and your
spouse?

Certain topics may not be appropriate in a spontaneous or stressful setting. Five minutes before your husband leaves for work is not the time to ask, "Honey, how do you think our children will turn out?" At times your spouse may be too tired or preoccupied to respond well if you say, "By the way, I've been meaning to talk to you about the latest credit card bill..." A couple of gracious "time-outs" can prevent an endless series of instant replays.

Ask about the timing. "Is this a good time to talk? If not, I'll be happy to wait." Once your spouse feels released from the pressure to talk at that moment, he or she may well pursue the conversation.

Schedule a better time. If your spouse raises an issue that you're not prepared to discuss, recommend another time when you can discuss it in an undistracted way. This will show that you genuinely desire to communicate and aren't just avoiding it. Commit to an alternative time. Just remember: If you put if off, you had better not forget to put it back on!

On the next two pages you will find a series of questions designed to deepen your marital intimacy and help you better serve your spouse. These will be most effective if you:

1. Select only two or three questions per discussion.

2. Give your spouse a couple of days to think about his/her answers.

3. Plan an evening to hear your spouse's answers.

4. Listen to your spouse's answers without interrupting or reacting.

5. Write out your spouse's answers and keep them where you can review them frequently.

6. Ask questions if you need clarification rather than "answering before you hear."

7. Appreciate the fact that if there are negative evaluations it may be as difficult for your spouse to share them as it will be for you to receive.

**Meditate on Proverbs
20:27 (NIV).** Ask God
to give you his "lamp"
so you can better know
your spouse.

8. Set goals and ask for accountability where change is needed. Check your progress periodically during times together.

9. Thank your spouse for his/her honesty and assistance in helping you follow Christ more closely.

10. Pray together. If forgiveness is needed in any area, ask for it—both from God and from your spouse. Ask for the grace and humility to love and serve your spouse in a way that honors God and extends his kingdom.

TWENTY QUESTIONS TO ASK YOUR WIFE

1. How can I make you feel more loved?
2. Do you feel you are the most important person in my life? If not, what makes you feel otherwise?
3. How can I better communicate how important you are to me?
4. How can I better understand when you need comfort, encouragement, or assurance? When is this most needed and how is it best expressed?
5. Am I gentle and assuring during a crisis?
6. How would you evaluate my leadership and responsiveness during conflict?
7. What three words would you use to describe our marriage? Give examples of each.
8. What are my strongest areas of leadership? Explain.
9. What are my weakest areas of leadership? Explain.
10. On a scale of 1–10 rate these three aspects of my communication skills:
    - Initiative
    - Content
    - Listening
11. If you could change one thing in me, what would it be?
12. On a scale of 1–10 how would you evaluate my role with our children?
    - Overall involvement
    - Teaching and training
    - Friendship
    - Example of relationship with Jesus
    - Discipline
        - consistent involvement
        - clear guidelines
        - full restoration
        - support for wife
13. How would you evaluate my pursuit of romance? How can I improve?
14. How would you evaluate my involvement in and oversight of our finances?
15. How would you evaluate my oversight of our schedule?
16. How would you evaluate my involvement in and concern for your…
    - Spiritual health and development
    - Physical health and development
    - Social health and development
    - Intellectual health and development
    - Recreational health and development
17. How would you evaluate my leadership in developing our sexual relationship and my concern for your sexual fulfillment?
18. Do I demonstrate a relationship with God that makes you feel secure?
19. What one area do you find most difficult to understand about me?
20. What do you see as my most admirable quality? How can I further develop this area of strength?

TWENTY QUESTIONS TO ASK YOUR HUSBAND

1. How can I make you feel more loved?
2. Do you feel you are the most important person in my life? If not, what makes you feel otherwise?
3. How can I better communicate how important you are to me?
4. How can I better understand when you need support, encouragement, or assurance? When is this most needed and how is it best expressed?
5. Am I responsive to your leadership during a crisis?
6. How would you evaluate my responsiveness and self-control during conflict?
7. What three words would you use to describe our marriage? Give examples of each.
8. What are my strongest areas as a wife?
9. What are my weakest areas as a wife?
10. On a scale of 1–10 rate these three aspects of my communication skills:
    - Timing (knowing when to initiate)
    - Content
    - Listening
11. If you could change one thing in me what would it be?
12. On a scale of 1–10 how would you evaluate my role with our children?
    - Overall involvement
    - Teaching and training
    - Friendship
    - Example of relationship with Jesus
    - Discipline
13. How would you evaluate my pursuit of romance? My responsiveness to your initiative? How can I improve?
14. How would you evaluate my use of finances?
15. How would you evaluate my ability to care for our home?
    - Planning
    - Prioritizing
    - Follow-through
16. How can I encourage and inspire you in your...
    - Spiritual health and development
    - Physical health and development
    - Social health and development
    - Intellectual health and development
    - Recreational health and development
17. How would you evaluate my responsiveness in our sexual relationship and my concern for your sexual fulfillment?
18. Does my relationship with God make you feel secure and free to lead?
19. What one area do you find most difficult to understand about me?
20. What do you see as my most admirable quality? How can I further develop this area of strength?

The busier your life gets, the fewer spontaneous opportunities you'll have to communicate. That's why it's so important to build these times into your schedule. Author Ralph Martin encourages couples to set aside between two and five hours per week specifically to talk, in addition to the regular flow of daily conversation. We've found the following options work well for certain couples:

- During meals (if you have no children)
- After children have gone to bed
- Lunch together if your work place and schedule allow it
- Going out once a week

You don't have to do anything exotic or expensive. Take a walk. Go for a drive in the country. Share a bag of popcorn or a cup of coffee. You can stay home if you want. The only requirement for effective communication is that your time be uninterrupted: no demands from children, no ringing phone, no bills to pay, no television. Be especially leery of television, that little square thing that sucks the life out of marriage. How much communication time is wasted while we sit glassy-eyed in front of the tube! If your viewing habits are firmly in check, that's fine. But if your TV is interfering with your communication, do something radical.

---

5 Take a few minutes to plan a date that would create a good context for communication. (Renting a video is out!) Be specific. Where would you go? What would you do? How much will it cost? Write down the details, then set a time when you can carry it out.

Once you set up a schedule that guarantees regular times for communication, guard it with your life. This must be a priority. Invest some time beforehand in planning what you will do and what you'll discuss. And wives, if you find your name listed in your husband's calendar, don't take it the wrong way. Don't think to yourself, *Oh,*

I'm just another of his appointments! He's making you a priority. If someone at work tries to schedule him at that time, he'll be able to say, "Sorry—I've got a very important meeting...with my wife."

To help stimulate your times of discussion, we've included at the end of this book a list of possible topics for conversation (see Appendix C, page 165) developed by a couple in our church. You may want to use this as a model for creating your own customized list of ideas. As you learn these things about each other you'll be better equipped to encourage one another, express appreciation, enhance your spouse's self-image, impart wisdom, and offer adjustment and correction when appropriate.

In Romans 12 Scripture describes what it means to be joined together as members of the Body of Christ. Much is said about forbearance, understanding, patience, rejoicing with those who rejoice, and bearing one another's burdens. Few of us would question these principles. What's funny, though, is that we try to apply those truths to our relationships within the church, but so often fail to implement them in our marriages. Yet this is for us! There's no better and more crucial place to obey Christ than at home with our spouse.

One in spirit, soul, and body. That's our Lord's vision for marriage. But there are two ways to merge. You can crash into each other at high speeds and fuse together from the sheer impact of the collision. We don't recommend that. Instead, use communication to build bridges, one after another, until the gap between you eventually disappears. ■

GROUP DISCUSSION

▶ According to the authors, what three ingredients must our communication contain? (Page 36)

▶ Can you think of specific examples when your communication failed because one or more of these was missing?

▶ Take a few minutes to practice gracious confrontation. The group leader will give one spouse a slip of paper describing the situation. (Example: "Your husband only brushes his teeth once a week" or "Your wife routinely insults you about the size of your earlobes.") Evaluate each other as you take turns "speaking the truth in love."

▶ What is one thing you do that helps you communicate effectively with your spouse?

▶ Are you aware of anything you do that hinders communication?

▶ To what degree does communication depend on an atmosphere of mutual acceptance?

▶ Do you have any recurring habits of speech you need to unlearn? (Page 40)

▶ Is there anything you're afraid to tell your spouse? What's the worst thing that could happen if you shared it with him/her?

▶ How can you as a couple insure that you have regular, scheduled times for communication?

RECOMMENDED READING   *To Understand Each Other* by Dr. Paul Tournier (Atlanta, GA: John Knox Press, ©1967)

Ten Weeks To A Better Marriage by Randall and Therese Cirner (Ann Arbor, MI: Servant Books, © 1985)

Answer to Warm-Up
(from page 35): D. 15 years. According to Richard Whitmire of Wycliffe Bible Translators, that much time is required just to translate the New Testament and *portions* of the Old Testament!

STORMY WEATHER

G A R Y   A N D   B E T S Y   R I C U C C I

SCRIPTURE TEXT Proverbs 12:18

WARM-UP Which country had the most hurricanes and tropical storms strike its shores during 1992?

A. China

B. Philippines

C. Mexico

D. Bangladesh

E. United States and its territories

(See page 65 for answer)

PERSONAL STUDY If you've been married more than a week or two, the following statement shouldn't surprise you. However, if you're in that pre-marital fantasyland of friction-free bliss—God's gracious way of insuring that couples make it all the way to the altar—you may resent what we're about to say. Maybe you'll be the exception, but thus far our informal research shows 100 percent of all married couples experience a common problem.

Conflict.

Jesus told a story about two men and two houses (Mt 7:24-28). One man was foolish, the other wise. One built his house on sand, the other built on rock. Yet they each faced rain, flood, and wind. Likewise, every marriage will encounter the elements of conflict. Sometimes there will be small conflicts, sometimes major storms. Some crises develop over a long period of time, and others blow up suddenly. But conflict in one form or another is inevitable. Why? Because we're sinners—and this side of heaven our sin and selfishness are going to be a problem.

Newlyweds often panic the first time they hit a heated conflict. "Nobody told me about this...Did I marry the wrong person?...What's wrong with our marriage?"

> **" The Bible does not teach that all conflict is bad; instead, it teaches that some differences are natural and beneficial. Since God has created us as unique individuals, human beings will often have different opinions, convictions, desires, perspectives, and priorities. Many of these differences are not inherently right or wrong; they are simply the result of God-given diversity and personal preferences. When handled properly, disagreements in these areas can stimulate productive dialogue, encourage creativity, promote helpful change, and generally make life more interesting.[1] "**
>
> **—Ken Sande**

There's no reason to fear. In fact, disagreement and conflict simply indicate that you and your spouse were created differently. There's certainly room for growth, but conflict is a normal part of any growing marriage.

Scripture tells us God created us in his image. How nice it would be if the script stopped there. You see, we are also called to be *conformed* to his image, which requires chiseling and pruning away the things in our character which dishonor God. Our Lord has sovereignly ordained that our refining process take place as we go *through* difficulties, not around them. The Bible is filled with examples of those who overcame as they passed *through* the wilderness, the Red Sea, the fiery furnace and ultimately the cross.

God doesn't protect Christians from their problems— he helps them walk victoriously *through* their problems. "A righteous man may have many troubles," wrote David, "but the Lord delivers him from them all" (Ps 34:19). What a promise! The path to peace, joy, and harmony in our marriages will take us through numerous conflicts. By the grace of God, those may be the very things that purify and strengthen our love for each other.

Success in marriage is measured not by the absence of conflict but by our response to conflict. So rather than waste time trying to attain the unattainable, let's learn how to appreciate the value of conflict and how to handle it redemptively when it occurs.

Meditate on John 16:33. Does this verse make you pessimistic or optimistic about the future?

Pulling You Apart or Together?

Colonial Williamsburg in Virginia is our favorite getaway place. We've made some wonderful memories there. But I (Betsy) remember one visit that seemed to be heading for disaster. Gary and I were walking down the street, and we were disagreeing about everything. At one point he stopped to take a picture of a tree. *What's the big deal about a tree?* I thought. *We've got plenty of those at home.* I stood there impatiently, considering the wisdom of marrying a man with an impulsive and artistic bent.

Then I sensed the Lord say, "Just look around." Lots of other couples were moving along the same street. But instead of walking hand in hand like Gary and I were, they were acting independently—looking at different buildings, exploring different sides of the street. Again I felt the Lord say, "Do you see what's happening? These couples are here to be distracted. You're here communicating. It's causing conflict, but it's pulling you closer because you're working it through."

Time after time God has had to remind us that when conflict does occur it can be very fruitful. That view doesn't come naturally. As the emotions begin to surge, neither of us is thinking, *Oh wonderful! I was hoping we could argue this evening! I'm being misunderstood— what an opportunity for us to get close!* Usually we're well into the conflict before that little revelation comes. Nevertheless it's true. If we can prevent conflict from forcing us apart, it actually serves to bond us together.

---

1 Take a moment to think about the most memorable conflict you and your spouse have ever had—either before or after your wedding. (One of ours was on our honeymoon!) Then answer the following questions:

■ How did it start?

■ How long did it last?

■ Did you do anything embarrassing during the conflict that you laugh about now?

For Further Study:
Read 1 Corinthians 3:10-13. What will God use ultimately to test the quality of our marriage? What effect does that have on your attitude toward building a better marriage?

Conflict's storms are valuable in that they test how you're building. They test a man's love and leadership as well as a woman's responsiveness and submission. Remember that panic you felt when your high school math teacher surprised you with a pop quiz? It seems like God often catches me (Gary) off guard: "Okay, Mr. Maturity, Mr. Understanding, Mr. Leadership—put your book away and pull out a pen and piece of paper." I can't count the times I've thought I had finally become the exemplary husband...only to discover after a few minutes of conflict how wrong I was! We won't instinctively appreciate these tests, but they are essential if we want a realistic assessment of the condition of our marriage.

Not only does conflict measure the current health of a marriage, but it gives each spouse a chance to grow and mature. Every disagreement is an opportunity for husbands to refine their leadership: to take initiative, to practice listening, and to discern the best course of action. Meanwhile the wife gets to develop her ability to respond with respect and self-control.

Have you ever seen the diet ads which show "before and after" shots of their happy clients? Those 75 pounds didn't just melt away. Hours of exercise and self-control shrunk that waistline, and you can bet that our happy client wasn't smiling then. Change is never effortless. As Charles Simpson has said, "Problems are the necessary hurdle between vision and reality."

Don't resent the problems in your marriage. Don't view conflict and the time needed to resolve conflict as an interruption, a distraction, or a failure. It's a necessary hurdle...not enjoyable, but necessary.

Over the years we've learned to resolve conflicts much more quickly. It used to take us days to work through an issue, in part because I (Betsy) lacked humility and self-control. But God challenged me to start cutting back on my response time. For me that has meant responding instead of reacting, restraining caustic comments, listening to his point of view and really trying to understand it, and asking forgiveness more quickly for my own sin.

Meditate on Proverbs 24:10. What does your behavior during conflict say about your level of character and spiritual strength?

2 Sam sits down to a gourmet meal, complete with candles and china, which his wife Elizabeth has made in honor of their third anniversary. After eating a few bites, Sam says, "You know, honey, you might want to experiment with Kraft macaroni and cheese some time. My mother used to fix it for us all the time!"

If you were in this couple's shoes, how long would it take you to resolve the conflict that's about to erupt?

❑ Less than an hour
❑ One to three hours
❑ All night
❑ All week
❑ As long as it takes to remove the candles from your iced tea!

How painful it is to discover a problem in your marriage. But how exciting to face that problem and overcome it together! We've had our share of conflicts, yet it's hard to remember most of them. That's because we do our best to deal with conflicts until they are thoroughly resolved. The hurt doesn't disappear immediately, but most of our conflicts are completely forgotten. They no longer clog the gears of our relationship. We can walk joyfully into the future without harboring any unresolved hurts from the past.

> **❝** A couple who are courageous enough always to say everything will without a doubt go through many upsets, but they will be able to build an ever more successful marriage.[2] **❞**
>
> —Paul Tournier

If your marriage is growing, it should take less and less time to work through conflict. Those committed to resolving conflict face a future as bright as the Lord himself.

That may be hard for you to believe right now. Perhaps your marriage has caused you such pain in the past that you doubt whether you even *have* a future. This next section should renew your hope and give you a strategy.

For Further Study:
Look up some of the rewards God promises in Revelation "to him who overcomes."

Four Fundamentals

By this point you're aware that conflict is a normal part of marriage. It's even a valuable part—if handled appropriately. Depending on our response, conflict will either reinforce or rip at our marriage.

There's nothing mystical about resolving conflict. What we're seeking to accomplish, as one dictionary defines it, is "to solve, to explain, to make clear, to remove." As simple as those definitions are, however, they rule out many of the techniques couples use—like ignoring problems, repressing emotions, or running away from issues. Nothing gets resolved that way. Our task is to explore painful issues, to clarify them, and ultimately to deal with them in such a way as to totally negate their influence on our relationship.

Resolving conflict requires that each spouse be willing to take a few basic steps. Let's look at these preliminaries before going any further.

Take responsibility for your own actions. Marital conflicts, like wars, begin with the assumption that someone is right and the other is wrong. We dig our trenches, roll out our tanks, and prepare to fight till the bloody end. As long as our objective is to defend our position and to zero in on our spouse's weaknesses, the battle will continue.

Now it's possible that your spouse really did commit some unimaginable offense. But it takes two to wage a war. What God wants you to focus on is your own contribution to the conflict. Was it your attitude? Timing? Selfishness? Withdrawal? Search your own heart, and let God search your spouse. Also, resist the urge to blame your spouse for your sinful reactions. He or she may provoke you, but God holds you accountable for your response. "Our behavior," writes Stephen R. Covey, "is a function of our *decisions*, not our conditions" (emphasis added).[3] Your spouse cannot cause sin in you. He or she simply helps you to discover what's already there. Marriage is the great revealer.

Pull out the log before plucking out specks. If we spent half as much time addressing our own faults as we spend judging our spouse's, we would experience very little conflict. First of all we wouldn't have time for anything else! Secondly, that humility would bring God's grace to prevent conflict. Jesus' words should make us pause before bringing a rebuke or criticism: "For in the same way you judge others you will be judged, and with the measure you use, it will be measured to you" (Mt 7:2).

Contrary to popular interpretation, Jesus' illustration of the log and the speck doesn't forbid making a judgment. Rather, it directs us to first search our own hearts and repent of all sin and self-righteousness so that we can then see clearly to help others be freed from the sin in their lives. "You hypocrite, first take the log out of your own eye, and then you will see clearly to take the speck out of your brother's eye" (Mt 7:5 NAS).

Meditate on 1 John 3:21. Apply this test before plucking out your spouse's specks. Perhaps you'll discover a log!

---

3 The following list is taken from the Bible's definition of love (1Co 13:4-7). Which of these *do not* currently characterize your conduct toward your spouse during conflict? (Check all that apply)

❑ Patient
❑ Kind
❑ Not envious
❑ Humble
❑ Polite
❑ Committed to truth
❑ Not selfish

❑ Not easily angered
❑ Forgiving
❑ Protective
❑ Trustful
❑ Hopeful
❑ Persevering

Confess your sin. Once we grasp the biblical principle that "God opposes the proud but gives grace to the humble" (Jas 4:6), confession is the only logical response. If you're unwilling to admit where you're wrong—regardless of the seriousness of your spouse's offense—God will oppose you. Count on it. No matter how eloquent or well-documented your defense, God will put his hand on your forehead and say, "This disagreement isn't going anywhere until you confess where *you* are wrong." (Gary: And if you look real close, you can still see the fingerprints just beneath my hairline!)

> ❝ Pride is at the root of almost all marital conflict. Pride is the part of us that cannot face being wrong. Thus we will not accept criticism, easily evaluate facts which suggest that we hold the wrong opinion, or allow for the possibility that there simply may be times when our partner is right and we are dead wrong. As long as being the strongest, the best, and the "rightest" is top priority, conflict will be destructive... What a burden is lifted when one no longer has to be right about everything.[4] ❞
>
> **—Gordon MacDonald**

Don't use your confession to reiterate your partner's faults: "I was wrong, but..." That three-letter word negates the impact of anything else you might say. Also, avoid making a mechanical or half-hearted confession. Your spouse will detect that instantly and then you'll have *another* conflict to worry about! We need God's help in this. His Spirit convicts us and helps us know just how our spouse feels when we are harsh, impatient, or bitter. That knowledge will produce genuine sorrow so we are more sensitive the next time a similar situation arises.

Ask forgiveness. Few conflicts arise in which one or the other spouse is completely innocent. Maybe you are only responsible for a small part of the mess, but you're responsible nonetheless. Don't just apologize. God expects you to ask forgiveness for your portion.

What if your spouse refuses to return the favor? That's difficult. It seems unfair, and you're tempted to become resentful (something else to confess!). But if you're going to play by God's rules, you take unilateral action, if necessary, to clean your own slate.

Rules for Resolving Conflict

With those fundamentals in place we're ready to press on toward resolution. Here's how to navigate the storms of disagreement without getting swamped by the waves.

Determine to understand. Our motive during conflict

is usually self-serving or mixed at best. Instead of trying to figure out what happened and why it happened, we begin to debate. We're more interested in winning the argument than discovering the truth. We want to prove we are right! How frequently we fit Solomon's description: "A fool finds no pleasure in understanding but delights in airing his own opinions" (Pr 18:2).

We've seen this in ourselves numerous times, but one of the most memorable events occurred years ago at a busy intersection. Because we drove on that street frequently, we knew the intersection had a sign posted which prohibited making a right-hand turn when the light was red. But on this particular day, I (Gary) noticed the sign had been removed. So I stopped, looked for oncoming traffic, then made the turn.

Betsy panicked. "Dear," she said, "you can't turn on red!"

Instead of explaining or saying something kind and reassuring, I got upset. To think that she would accuse me, with my impeccable driving record and skill, of violating a traffic ordinance! So in my own gracious way I drove down the street, went around the corner, and came back to the light.

> " As long as a man is preoccupied primarily with being understood by his wife, he is miserable, overcome with self-pity, the spirit of demanding, and bitter withdrawal. As soon as he becomes preoccupied with understanding her, seeking to understand that which he had not before understood, and with his own wrongdoing in not having understood her, then the direction taken by events begins to change.[5] "
>
> —Paul Tournier

"Look," I said. "There's no sign!"

My triumph lasted only a second; it was clear I had hurt Betsy. It's obvious now that I wasn't trying to resolve anything when I made that U-turn. Had I cared about her concerns I would have taken the time to explain my actions. But I just wanted to defend myself, to prove I was right. As it turned out, I merely proved how wrong I was.

So many conflicts can be extinguished if we'll rephrase the basic question—not "Who is right?" but "What is right?" Because conflict stirs up self-centered emotions, the waters of reason quickly get muddied. We want to get even, to vindicate ourselves. We want somebody to pay for our pain. But we can't resolve conflict until we exercise self-control over our emotions and take an objective look at the problem. Do you know why your wife said that? Do you know why your husband did that? Are you *sure,* or are you making an assumption? "He who answers before listening—that is his folly and his shame" (Pr 18:13). First

For Further Study:
Read 1 Peter 3:7. Ineffectual prayers are a good indicator that you're failing to understand your spouse. Ask God to reveal any areas where you may be inconsiderate. Husbands should take the lead in this, but there's a lesson here for wives as well.

56

establish the facts, then begin to discuss what you felt and why you felt that way.

If one of us "loses" in a conflict, we both lose. On the other hand, both sides win when conflict leads to deeper levels of understanding.

---

4 Joe said he would be home from work at 5:15. His wife Josephine, who has been home all day with two small children, scheduled dinner for 5:30 so they would have time to eat and clean up before guests arrive at 6:30. Joe walks in the door at 6:05. What words would you put in their mouths to help them resolve the situation? (Each has just two sentences.)

Josephine:

Joe:

Josephine:

Joe:

Determine to remain calm. To see a situation clearly you have to see it calmly, and that requires self-control. It's a simple choice between being wise or being foolish: "A fool is hotheaded and reckless...A patient man has great understanding, but a quick-tempered man displays folly" (Pr 14:16,29). As we've mentioned already, we need God's grace to subordinate our emotions. But we also need to realize that quarrels depend more on the people involved than on the issues. How can we blame an issue for our bitterness, our anger, our resentment, or whatever else might come spilling out? Staying calm requires character, and character comes as the grace of God teaches us to trust, obey, and conform to Christ.

Someone has said that it's tough to be objective when you're the object. If you take conflict personally, you lose sight of the issue and conclude that *you* are the issue. Often I (Betsy) am tempted to run when Gary confronts me on something. I can misinterpret his rebuke, no matter how gently worded, as rejection. And that usually halts

Meditate on Proverbs 29:11. Where do you draw the line between expressing your emotions and venting your anger?

our progress toward restoration. At times we will stop the conversation there for a few minutes so I can go to God and regain perspective, reminding myself that Gary's confrontation is a loving adjustment, not a personal attack. If this kind of pause will help, give it a try. But please don't use it as an excuse to reinforce your defenses!

> " We tend to follow a natural pattern when we've been offended. Mentally, we are more alert to the flaws of the offender. Emotionally, we feel estranged. Physically, we avoid that person. And spiritually we close out the person (Pr 15:13).[6] "
>
> —**Gary Smalley**

Most people don't wait until they're soaked before they open their umbrella. Likewise, it's probably not a good idea to wait until the conflict to start refining your character. By meditating on relevant Scripture and practicing patience and self-control while your marriage is peaceful, you'll be far more calm when the storm hits.

Husbands, determine to lead the conversation. There's no area where I (Gary) am more aware of my need for the grace of God. Leadership requires a touch both tough and tender, forged of steel but lined with velvet. Men, it is our responsibility to insure that conflicts move toward resolution, and that takes leadership and humility. Keep the main issue in focus without getting distracted. Sometimes your wife would prefer not to communicate. Maybe you feel the same way. But unless you steer the conversation your problem will get worse.

Your leadership is only as good as your motive. Are you trying to serve your wife or serve yourself? Are you dominating the conversation and making demands, or humbly showing her respect? Are you demonstrating self-control? She should have clear evidence of your love and care as you draw her out and explore each concern.

Leading a conversation effectively involves paying close attention to small but important details. Should you sit beside her or across from her? Touch or not touch? Talk or be quiet? Laugh or not laugh? (Whatever you do, don't get that one wrong!) Leave her alone or gently persist? The approach that works wonders today may cause an explosion tomorrow. During one conflict (I'm sure it was many, many years ago) Betsy said she needed to be alone for awhile. The moment of decision! Should I pick door number one: Let her go? Or door number two: Insist that we continue? I said I understood and let her go. Bingo! Success! Later she returned from the bedroom and we were able to work things out.

Believe it or not, the very next day we had another conflict. This time Betsy didn't ask, she simply walked back to our bedroom and shut the door. So I thought, *No problem...door number one.* Wrong! That was yesterday, pal! After a couple of hours Betsy emerged, tearfully wondering why I hadn't pursued her. Men, don't ask me and don't try to figure these things out. Take my advice: ask God...*every* time.

Every conflict has a different dynamic, even if you're talking about the same issue. Don't bother looking for a technique or formula—to lead well you must rely on the guidance of the Holy Spirit.

Wives, determine to participate and respond. Early in our marriage, I (Betsy) took advantage of opportunities to press Gary's "buttons." For example, if he was trying to resolve a conflict, I knew I could upset him by saying, "I don't care. I just don't care."

During one disagreement I got deeply offended and retaliated with indifference. But then I got a mental image of a sailboat being tossed by rough seas. The husband had the rudder and it was the wife's job to control the sail, making sure it was positioned to catch the wind so the boat could get out of the storm. Yet this woman had her hands folded and was sitting down—a perfect picture of my attitude. At that point I felt God tell me, "If you don't participate in this conflict and the boat goes over, you're going over with it. You're part of this thing! If you don't do your job, you're sunk."

Meditate on Proverbs 16:32. Does this imagery motivate you to battle for self-control?

Women, as Christ's followers we have no option but to respond in the midst of conflict, and respond with self-control. I'm not saying that will be easy. When we get rattled, the emotions come flying out in all directions. Those are difficult to control. In fact, once I was listening to a tape and was shocked to hear the speaker say, "There's nothing you can do about your emotions." *What?!* I thought to myself. *Am I off the hook?* I should have known better. This is a paraphrase, but his next statement went something like this: "What you *can* do something about is your thoughts, your actions, and your words. Your emotions can go in every direction. Quit focusing on how you feel! Just respond by taking charge of your thoughts, words, and actions, and your emotions will get in line."

At times during conflict I allow my emotions to pull me where I should not go. And it can be an exhausting trip as I am jerked around by feelings of anger, rejection, misunderstanding, and fear. I have found it so liberating to

Meditate on Proverbs 15:18. Are conflicts shorter or longer as a result of your participation?

know that I am not at the mercy of my emotions! As I direct my thoughts, words, and actions in obedience to God's Word, my emotions will eventually follow. I'm not saying it's easy, but it does work!

Determine to listen without interrupting. Conflicts are often more emotional than logical. Are you willing to be a "dumping ground"? I (Gary) have seen how important it is that Betsy feel free to communicate her emotions. I give her that freedom by listening. The extent to which I listen determines the extent to which she feels understood. Sometimes I have to bite my tongue to keep from interrupting, especially when I think I've got it all figured out. But if I wait until she has expressed herself fully and the dust of emotion settles, I'm better able to respond and she's better able to receive.

On the other hand, as important as it is to express one's emotions, neither spouse has the liberty to become abusive or to sin. Bible teacher Bill Gothard says we can never let hurt become an excuse for a lack of self-control. If Betsy's sharing turns into an emotional free-fall, I'm prepared to intervene and bring things back into focus. But that can only work if I have previously demonstrated my care and understanding.

> " In order really to understand, we need to listen, not to reply. We need to listen long and attentively. In order to help anybody to open his heart, we have to give him time, asking only a few questions, as carefully as possible, in order to help him better explain his experience. Above all we must not give the impression that we know better than he does what he must do. Otherwise we force him to withdraw. [7] "
>
> —Paul Tournier

Determine not to hurt your spouse. Think of some of the most painful conversations you've had with your spouse, the ones you're glad nobody else heard. Would you ever talk to your boss that way? Your pastor? Your neighbor? It's amazing how we take liberties within the confines of our home that we wouldn't take anywhere else. When our spouse hurts us, we retaliate without restraint. But when others hurt us, we typically exercise self-control. Why should there be a difference?

It helps me (Gary) to remember that Betsy didn't have to marry me. She volunteered freely. When I see her as a gift (rather than a given) I am less inclined to hurt her and more inclined to serve her.

5 What things do you consistently say or do during conflict that hurt your spouse?

What does your spouse say or do during conflict that hurts you?

We've already taken you through two chapters on communication, but it won't hurt to reiterate the impact our words have. The words used in a conflict will be remembered long after the issue is forgotten.

Take the word "ridiculous," for example, or the phrase "a waste of time." Both surfaced during the infamous and humorous tuna fish incident. I (Betsy) was making our Sunday lunch and asked Gary to help me squeeze the water out of the tuna fish. He did—but not well enough. You see, I'm pretty particular about having dry tuna fish.

"Gary, could you squeeze the rest of the water out?" I asked.

"This is ridiculous," he answered, feigning irritation.

"But I like it that way," I said.

"This is a waste of time."

"It's not a waste of time to *me!*"

And so it unfolded, with our bemused children looking on, wide-eyed. This was a lighthearted exchange, but these words used in anger would have been destructive.

Some couples make the opposite mistake by withholding legitimate correction in an effort not to hurt each other. That's dishonest, and can actually do greater harm. Scripture says, "Wounds from a friend can be trusted...He who rebukes a man will in the end gain more favor than he who has a flattering tongue" (Pr 27:6, 28:23).

Our tongues have "the power of life and death" (Pr 18:21). Yet Jesus taught that life-giving tongues draw their inspiration from deeper down: "Out of the overflow of the heart the mouth speaks" (Mt 12:34). A change in

For Further Study:
Every couple should take time to research the following verses: Proverbs 10:19, 12:18, 13:3, 15:1, 15:18, 16:32, 17:27, 18:17, and 25:15. Write them out. Hang them up where you can see them. Meditate on them until they shape your patterns of communication.

our speech—or in anything else—must begin in the heart. That's why this book depends entirely on Scripture as the pattern and final authority for marriage. We strengthen our hearts and renew our minds by filling them with the truth of God's Word. We should make it our goal to see the reservoir of our heart overflowing with love, acceptance, grace, and wisdom. That way, when the emotional waters are turbulent, what overflows in our speech will be life-giving and not lethal.

Determine to extend genuine forgiveness. Once you and your spouse have discussed all the issues pertaining to the conflict, often someone will need to ask forgiveness. If that's you, do it humbly and thoroughly. If your spouse is the offender, recognize that you have your own work ahead. No matter how much you have been hurt, no matter how much you still question your spouse's motives or sincerity, you must extend forgiveness. Unconditional forgiveness. "Be kind and compassionate to one another, forgiving each other, just as in Christ God forgave you" (Eph 4:32).

God knows how difficult this is. He forgave his enemies while they were putting the nails in his hands. Through him we receive grace to say to our spouse, "I put this conflict behind me. I will not judge or resent you. In light of God's mercy and forgiveness toward me, I forgive you without hesitation. I refuse to evaluate our relationship on the basis of what just happened. It's over. Now let's learn from this and press on so that we can respond differently in the future."

If there are heaps of unresolved conflict in your marriage that you've never discussed, we don't advise you to dig everything up at once. But start talking about these things. Bring them out in the light. Otherwise they will fester inside, poisoning your relationship with your spouse and with God.

---

6 Which of the following movie titles comes closest to describing your worst conflict ever?

❑ *Night of the Living Dead*
❑ *King Kong Meets Godzilla*
❑ *Nightmare on Elm Street*
❑ *Psycho*
❑ *War of the Worlds*

Betsy and I have gotten in the habit of reviewing our conflicts. Within a day or two after resolving a conflict we will bring it back out on the table and talk through it again. Because our emotions have usually subsided by this point, we find it much easier to understand our responses and learn from our sin and mistakes. It may seem like this would contradict the principle of leaving issues behind, but it doesn't. Actually, it enables us to further humble ourselves, understand each other, and resolve these issues more completely. It also solidifies our intent to be more sensitive and less selfish in the future.

> ❝ The Bible teaches that we should see conflict neither as an inconvenience nor as an occasion for selfish gain, but rather as an opportunity to demonstrate the presence and power of God.[8] ❞
>
> —Ken Sande

Determine to seek help if reconciliation is unattainable. At times one spouse or the other may develop a pattern of behavior that doesn't seem to respond to resolution or reconciliation. Despite repeated conflicts over the same issue, there's no change.

There may also be times when you reach an impasse in your efforts to resolve a conflict. One or the other of you, or both, have dug in and refuse to budge. Pride goes up and communication shuts down. If not dealt with, this can be highly destructive.

I (Betsy) admire the way Gary has protected me from these kinds of situations. Years ago he told me, "If you feel at any time that I am not responding to a conflict or if it's lasting too long, I give you permission to call C.J. and get him involved." C.J. is senior pastor in the church we serve—he also happens to be my brother. Gary's offer gave me a deep sense of security, and a new respect for him. I could see he really cared about our marriage. His willingness to risk embarrassment, if necessary, to prevent an impasse or prolonged disobedience is wonderful proof of his love.

Men, we can even go a step further and make a commitment to get help ourselves when we reach an impasse or prolonged conflict. Humbling yourself before others takes real courage. Yet authentic Christianity leaves us no other choice. God has established his Church knowing how much we need each other to become like him. Every couple should prayerfully seek and get actively involved in a local church where the pastors and leadership demonstrate the joy and sanctity of covenant love in marriage. Please don't neglect this. This is certainly another applica-

Meditate on Ephesians 4:14-16. Is it possible to carry out these verses in isolation?

tion of the biblical principle that "two are better than one" (Ecc 4:9).

Getting Better Every Year

We touched on this briefly at the beginning of the chapter, but we want to close with a reminder that conflict can be very fruitful. When we successfully resolve a disagreement we're doing far more than avoiding a storm. We're becoming like Christ. We are maturing. As conflict and communication change us, we won't have to face the same issues year after year. (Don't worry about getting bored—there will be new issues!) Conflict resolution also draws us closer to each other, resulting in deeper levels of understanding, humility, and intimacy. Each conflict happily concluded brings us a step nearer to oneness.

So many couples spend their lives avoiding conflict. They choose peace at any price—a price much higher than they realize. It's challenging and can be painful, but in the end conflict resolution is deeply rewarding.

We have had the privilege of serving so many couples who through grace, faith, and obedience have turned from strife and misery to harmony and intimacy. God is faithful and there is no situation beyond his ability to restore when both partners want to do God's will. Let that stir great hope and anticipation. One day as you look back over the road your own marriage has traveled, you'll be able to say, "Look what we've come through! We even survived the tuna fish! By the grace of God, no disagreement or misunderstanding will ever be able to break the bonds of our love." ■

> ❝ Deeply ingrained patterns of avoidance are nothing more than relational games...Probably the most obvious avoidance strategy is simply to never bring the issue up for discussion. Never means never. You just never talk about sex in your home; or question where the marriage is going; or express your concern about needs that are not getting met; or how in-laws are interfering in divisive ways; or, for that matter, anything else of significance...Sometimes you even feel very justified in avoiding issues in this manner:
>
> "Think of the hostility that would be created if we discussed it."
>
> "I'm really helping to preserve my marriage by not bringing it up."
>
> "It wouldn't get settled anyway."
>
> One counselor has said, "If you can think of a subject that you and your spouse have not talked about recently, it is probably the very thing you need to deal with the most." Just because something isn't discussed by people does not mean that it is not standing between them.[9] ❞
>
> —**Donald R. Harvey**

▶ If you wanted to make your spouse really angry during a conflict, what would you do?

▶ According to the authors, "Success in marriage is measured not by the absence of conflict but by our response to conflict" (Page 50). Do you agree or disagree?

▶ Re-read the quote from Charles Simpson on page 52. How do you interpret his statement?

▶ What would you do if your spouse was unwilling to resolve a conflict?

▶ Read Romans 14:9-13. Do you tend to judge your spouse? If God judged you the same way, what would the verdict be?

▶ Could an absence of conflict indicate that a marriage is *unhealthy?*

▶ What determines whether or not we've won an argument? (Page 57)

▶ Do you find it hard to control your emotions during conflict? Impossible?

▶ When is it appropriate to back off during a conflict? When is it appropriate to press in?

▶ Has this study changed your attitude toward conflict?

RECOMMENDED READING

The Peacemaker by Ken Sande (Grand Rapids, MI: Baker Book House, © 1991)

Men And Women by Larry Crabb (Grand Rapids, MI: Zondervan Publishing House, © 1991)

Answer to Warm-Up
(from page 49): E. United States and its territories. Did your marriage get hit by its own "Hurricane Andrew" that year? (Source: National Weather Service)

HUSBANDS: LEAD WITH LOVE

GARY RICUCCI

SCRIPTURE TEXT Ephesians 5:25-33

WARM-UP Which NFL quarterback/receiver duo set individual team records in the same season for most yards passed/received?

A. Joe Theismann / Art Monk

B. Terry Bradshaw / John Stallworth

C. Joe Montana / Jerry Rice

D. Dan Marino / Mark Clayton

E. George Blanda / Charley Hennigan

(See page 84 for answer)

PERSONAL STUDY "When you hear about how much God expects of you as a husband, you're gonna' want to quit." That statement has stuck with me since I first heard it at a conference in Montreat, North Carolina in 1974. It echoes in my mind as I set out to communicate in this study what Scripture says about the role of a husband.

The roles of a husband and wife are treated separately in this book because God has created them to be distinctly different. John Piper comments on this distinction in the book *Recovering Biblical Manhood and Womanhood*:

When the Bible teaches that men and women fulfill different roles in relation to each other, charging man with a unique leadership role, it bases this differentiation not on temporary cultural norms but on permanent facts of creation...In the Bible, differentiated roles for men and women are never traced back to the fall of man and woman into sin. Rather, the foundation of this differentiation is traced back to the way things were in Eden before sin warped our relationships. Differentiated roles were corrupted, not created, by the fall. They were created by God.[1]

This fundamental truth is essential to the development of a thriving marriage.

God has very specific—and demanding—expectations of married men. These can appear intimidating until we understand that God will give us the grace to do all he commands us to do. As Andrew Murray wrote a century ago, "Every commandment from God is a promise." The Lord himself promises to help us provide the love, joy, peace, and order he requires (and we desire) in our marriage. A successful marriage is possible because all things are possible with him.

What is the man's role in building the kind of marriage God intends? How do we uniquely contribute to a marriage that honors Jesus Christ, serves our wives, builds the Church, and reaches the lost?

Understand and Honor

In a single verse, Peter pinpoints two of a husband's primary responsibilities: "You husbands, likewise, live with your wives *in an understanding way*, as with a weaker vessel, since she is a woman; and *grant her honor* as a fellow heir of the grace of life, so that your prayers may not be hindered" (1Pe 3:7 NAS). More than good ideas, these directives are foundational to biblical male leadership and any subsequent success and harmony in marriage.

To better understand what Peter means by living "in an understanding way," consider two other translations of the same phrase. The New International Version says "be considerate as you live with your wives." The King James Version says "dwell with them according to knowledge." This refers to experiential knowledge, not mere information. Who is this woman you've married? What goes on inside her mind and heart? What are her fears? Her dreams? Answering those questions will require

TEN INGREDIENTS OF UNDERSTANDING

- A desire to understand
- Total honesty (without rudeness)
- Courage to be vulnerable
- Ability to listen patiently
- Humility
- Love and commitment
- Acceptance and respect
- A desire to help
- Sensitivity to your spouse's past
- Submission to Jesus Christ

Meditate on Proverbs 4:7-9. Here's all the motivation you should need to pursue understanding!

that you study your wife and take an interest in all she thinks and does. Don't assume you know what she feels or what motivates her. She is a mystery. Just when you think you have figured her out, she will do or say something that you could never have predicted.

---

1 Complete this sentence: *The most surprising thing my wife has ever said or done was when she...*

It takes patience and perseverance to understand our wives, and they undoubtedly feel the same about us. By way of example (purely hypothetical, of course), suppose it's Sunday night and you're looking over the weekly calendar together just before going to bed. To you the schedule is more than manageable: a small group Bible study, one evening of overtime, a birthday party for your six-year-old son, a night class, and dinner for your parents' anniversary. No problem. Yet suddenly your wife reacts emotionally. What do you do?

> **"** People so very different by nature are nevertheless made to complement each other, that through each other they may discover so much of what they've not known or sensed before. This is one of the purposes of marriage.[2] **"**
>
> **—Paul Tournier**

Tell her she's overreacting? Tell her she's not supporting your leadership? Tell her she's in unbelief? (This is a good one if you've got nothing to do for the next two or three hours!)

I recommend you not tell her anything. Instead, take some time to ask questions and listen. Find out what's really bothering her. There's probably a good reason for her response.

Please don't begin your quest for understanding with an abrupt, "Now what's wrong?!" Your wife must know that her counsel, thoughts, and feelings are valuable to you, and that you will take whatever time is necessary to consider her point of view. After talking, if you see that your planning was unwise, admit it and thank your wife for her wisdom. If together you determine the schedule is workable (which in the scenario described above is unlikely), your discussion must still lead you to the actual cause of her reaction. Fatigue? PMS? Feelings of failure? Fear of your parents? Don't flippantly dismiss her feelings then offer a casual word of encouragement. The only way you will be able to help her broaden her perspective of the situation is to first understand her feelings.

Reaching the root may not be easy. You may have to conduct an aggressive but gentle pursuit before she shares her true feelings. In order to understand her, though, you must engage her in ongoing communication.

The second fundamental need Peter mentions is a need for honor. Some men think they're meeting this need merely by avoiding negative behavior—being harsh, perhaps, or reacting in anger. But honor isn't passive, it's active. We honor our wives by demonstrating our esteem and respect: complimenting them in public, affirming their gifts, abilities, and accomplishments, and declaring our appreciation for all they do. Honor not expressed is not honor. Gratitude not expressed is not gratitude.

Meditate on Romans 12:10. Can you think of one specific way in which you honor your wife above yourself?

When Scripture calls the woman "a weaker vessel," the phrase itself implies honor. Consider Paul's description of the body in 1 Corinthians 12: "Those parts of the body that seem to be weaker are indispensable, and the parts that we think are less honorable we treat with special honor" (v.22,23). The description is meant to produce honor and respect.

Peter goes on to describe a cause and effect relationship: if we dishonor our wives, our prayers will be hindered. Mark this down. If you find particular prayer requests going unanswered, perhaps you are not honoring your wife and living with her in an understanding way. God won't let you mistreat his daughter without consequences. They may not be immediate, but they are inevitable.

---

2 Listed below are some common ways husbands can honor their wives in public. Check any of these you do on a regular basis:

❏ Pay attention when she is speaking

❏ Help her on with her coat

❏ Pull out her chair at the table

❏ Carry her luggage, books, etc.

❏ Open her car door

❏ Say "thank you," "excuse me," etc.

Servant Leadership

Once we've made the commitment to understand and honor our wives, we're in a good position to handle a third marital responsibility: the responsibility to lead.

"Now I want you to realize," Paul wrote the Corinthians, "that the head of every man is Christ, and the head of the woman is man, and the head of Christ is God" (1Co 11:3). This verse (and other sections of Scripture) tells us husbands have a God-given privilege, responsibility, and authority to lead.

Before you get impressed with your status, note the order in which Paul made his statement above. Leadership begins with the fact that Christ is the head of every man. That should give our wives security. If they know we're submitted to Jesus Christ and that our desire is to obey his Word, walk humbly before him, and allow his mighty hand to rest on our lives through the spiritual authority of others, it gives them great confidence in our leadership. If they don't see us submitting to Christ, they will find it difficult to submit respectfully and willingly to us. They're still obliged to do that, but it's far easier when they know God is pre-eminent in our lives.

> **“** In reflecting on the nature of the family crisis in this country today, I have become convinced that behind it lies another, deeper crisis. It is a crisis that has received relatively little attention. The deeper crisis I refer to is quite simply a crisis of American manhood, that is, a crisis in what it means to be a man...[3] **”**
> —**Paul Vitz**

As Christ is the head of man, so man is the head of woman. The position is not a matter of worth or value. If headship were earned, our wives probably would have taken over the role long ago. No—as John Piper stated at the beginning of the study, the man is head of the woman because God sovereignly ordered creation this way. Our role didn't originate with a certain culture or with Paul the apostle or with Dr. James Dobson; it originated in the Godhead and was revealed when the world began.

John Piper's treatment of a husband's leadership role is simply outstanding. He defines masculinity in chapter one of *Recovering Biblical Manhood and Womanhood*:

At the heart of mature masculinity is a sense of benevolent responsibility to lead, provide for and protect women in ways appropriate to a man's differing relationships.[4]

He goes on to unfold the meaning and applications of that definition. In my opinion these biblical truths could not be stated any more accurately or directly. So rather than give you second best, I've asked permission to excerpt the rest of this section directly from Piper's chapter. Read these paragraphs carefully—let them redefine, where necessary, your understanding of the husband's role.

Mature masculinity expresses itself not in the demand to be served, but in the strength to serve and to sacrifice for the good of woman. Jesus said, "Let the greatest among you become as the youngest and the leader as one who serves" (Lk 22:26). Leadership is not a demanding demeanor. It is moving things forward to a goal. If the goal is holiness and Heaven, the leading will have the holy aroma of Heaven about it—the demeanor of Christ.

Thus after saying that "the husband is the head of the wife as Christ is the head of the church," Paul said, "Husbands, love your wives as Christ loved the church and *gave himself up for her*, that he might sanctify her" (Eph 5:23,25). Jesus led his bride to holiness and heaven on the *Calvary* road. He looked weak, but he was infinitely strong in saying NO to the way of the world. So it will be again and again for mature men as they take up the responsibility to lead.

> 66 The fact that husbands are to treat their wives with "respect" does not mean that the wife, who has less authority, is less important. Peter's telling husbands that their wives are joint heirs of the grace of life reminds them that, even though they have been given greater authority within marriage, their wives are still equal to them in spiritual privilege and eternal importance.[5] 99
>
> —**Wayne Grudem**

Mature masculinity does not assume the authority of Christ over woman, but advocates it. The leadership implied in the statement, "The husband is the head of the wife *as Christ is the head of the church*" (Eph 5:23), is not a leadership that gives to the man all the rights and authority that Christ has. The analogy between Christ and the husband breaks down if pressed too far, first because, unlike Christ, all men sin. Christ never has to apologize to his church. But husbands must do this often.

Moreover, unlike Christ, a husband is not preparing a bride merely for himself but for another, namely Christ. He does not merely act as Christ, but also for Christ. At this point he must not be Christ to his wife lest he be a traitor to Christ. Standing in the place of Christ must include a renunciation of the temptation to be Christ. And that means leading his wife forward to depend not on him but on Christ. And practically, that rules out belittling supervision and fastidious oversight. She also stands or falls before her own master, Jesus Christ…

Mature masculinity does not have to initiate every action, but feels the responsibility to provide a general pattern of initiative. In a family the husband does not do all the thinking and planning. His leadership is to take responsibility *in general* to initiate and carry through the spiritual and moral planning for family life. I say "in general" because "in specifics" there will be many times and many areas of daily life where the wife will do all kinds of planning and initiating. But there is a general tone and pattern of initiative that should develop which is sustained by the husband.

For example, the leadership pattern would be less than biblical if the wife in general was having to take the initiative in prayer at mealtime, and get the family out of bed for worship on Sunday morning, and gather the family for devotions, and discuss what moral standards will be required of the children, and confer about financial priorities, and talk over some neighborhood ministry possibilities, etc. A wife may initiate the discussion and planning of any one of these, but if she becomes the one who senses the general responsibility for this pattern of initiative while her husband is passive, something contrary to biblical masculinity and femininity is in the offing…

For Further Study:
Find the one characteristic of great leadership described in each of the following verses: Zechariah 9:9; Matthew 11:29; 1 Thessalonians 2:7; and 1 Timothy 3:3.

---

3 In the space below, ask yourself (and answer) the following question: *What do I do that hinders my wife from responding confidently and joyfully to my leadership in the home?* Within the next day or two, ask your wife for her response.

Mature masculinity accepts the burden of the final say in disagreements between husband and wife, but does not presume to use it in every instance. In a good marriage decision-making is focused on the husband, but is not unilateral. He seeks input from his wife and often adopts her ideas. This is implied in the love that governs the relationship (Eph 5:25), in the equality of personhood implied in being created in the image of God (Ge 1:27), and in the status of being fellow-heirs of the grace of life (1Pe 3:7). Unilateral decision-making is not usually a mark of good leadership. It generally comes from laziness or insecurity or inconsiderate disregard.

On the other hand dependence on team input should not go to the point where the family perceives a weakness of indecision in the husband. And both husband and wife should agree on the principle that the husband's decision should rightly hold sway if it does not involve sin. However, this conviction does not mean that a husband will often use the prerogative of "veto" over the wishes of his wife or family. He may, in fact, very often surrender his own preference for his wife's where no moral issue is at stake. His awareness of his sin and imperfection will guard him from thinking that following Christ gives him the ability of Christ to know what's best in every detail.

> 66 Mutual submission does not mean that the husband and wife take turns being the head of the home. That is the man's permanent assignment. It does mean that the husband demonstrates and models the concept of submission in his own life when the situation calls for such a response. Mutual submission is just another way of describing servant leadership for the husband and loving submission for the wife. *It is at the core of both biblical headship and biblical submission.*[6] 99
>
> —**Steve Farrar**

Nevertheless, in a well-ordered biblical marriage both husband and wife acknowledge in principle that, if necessary in some disagreement, the husband will accept the burden of making the final choice...

Mature masculinity recognizes that the call to leadership is a call to repentance and humility and risk-taking. We are all sinners. Masculinity and femininity have been distorted by our sin. Taking up the responsibility to lead must therefore be a careful and humble task. We must admit as men that historically there have been grave abuses. In each of our lives we have ample cause for contrition at our passivity or our domination. Some have neglected their wives and squandered their time in front of the television or putzing around in the garage or going away too often with the guys to hunt or fish or bowl. Others have been too possessive, harsh, domineering, and belittling, giving the impression through act and innuendo that wives are irresponsible or foolish.

For Further Study:
Read 2 Corinthians 8:8.
Would your love for your
wife pass the test Paul
describes here?

We should humble ourselves before God for our failures and for the remaining tendency to shirk or overstep our responsibilities. The call to leadership is not a call to exalt ourselves over any woman. It is not a call to domineer, or belittle or put woman in her place. She is, after all, a fellow-heir of God and destined for a glory that will one day blind the natural eyes of every man (Mt 13:43). The call to leadership is a call to humble oneself and take the responsibility to be a servant-leader in ways that are appropriate to every differing relationship to women.

It is a call to risk getting egg on our faces; to pray as we have never prayed before; to be constantly in the Word; to be more given to planning, more intentional, more thoughtful, less carried along by the mood of the moment; to be disciplined and ordered in our lives; to be tenderhearted and sensitive; to take the initiative to make sure there is a time and a place to talk to her about what needs to be talked about; and to be ready to lay down our lives the way Christ did if that is necessary.[7]

God's Good and Perfect Gift

As Piper mentioned in the previous section, responsible leadership means recognizing your wife's gifts and strengths and involving her in decisions that affect your marriage and family. Men, remember that "helpmeet" is as much a reflection of our considerable need as it is of a wife's position in divine order. Only the most foolish husband would fail to draw upon the abilities and wisdom of his wife.

People will often remark that even though Betsy and I have four young children and many ministry responsibilities, there is a very evident peace and orderliness in our home. And here's why—it's a result of Betsy's intimacy with God, as well as her initiative, creativity, and day-to-day oversight of our household affairs. I recognize that every family and situation is different, but I want to offer a few glimpses of how authority is shared and delegated in the Ricucci household.

Because she is with the children all day, Betsy is best able to observe their specific character needs during any given season of time. While I might occasionally refine the issue, she establishes the focal point of their training. It's my privilege to oversee and enforce that training.

Within our mutually agreed upon budget, Betsy has full liberty to make purchases for herself, our children, and our home, and to give to others as she becomes aware of needs. Very simply, I trust her. I want her to flourish in her gifts and identity as a homemaker. Betsy also takes direct responsibility for decorating our home, extending hospitality, caring for women in our sphere of ministry, and several aspects of our planning and scheduling.

I have great confidence in Betsy's skill and ability, and I am deeply grateful for her support. Her commitment to the Lord and to me in my role as her husband makes it easy to entrust so many aspects of our life to her care and oversight. Even when she disagrees with me or questions my decisions, she does it in a respectful way that reinforces my leadership. (And I usually wind up making a wiser decision.) Without her initiative and input, our household would suffer dramatically.

> ** ** The vast majority of men have wives who want their husbands to win. She is on your team. When a man begins to understand that, he views his wife in a new way. Gentlemen, your wife is a strategic gift to you! She has eyes that see what you don't, a mind that assimilates information from a different perspective, a heart with sensitivities you do not possess, and a personality with strengths that offset your weaknesses. That's a built-in protection for you. That's why you must tap into her perspective as you lead your family.[8] **"**
>
> —Steve Farrar

As long as the husband provides the kind of leadership John Piper described, his wife has virtually unlimited potential for initiative without trespassing the boundaries of God-given authority. But men, if you create a leadership vacuum—due to ignorance, indifference, or foolish neglect—more often than not your wife will try to fill it. You may think she's usurping your authority and become resentful. The fact is, she's simply trying to act responsibly in the face of your irresponsibility!

Meditate on Matthew 20:25-28. This passage describes two kinds of rulers. Which kind are you?

Sadly, numerous husbands have abdicated their position of authority in the home. That's why I want to close this section with a sobering look at one passage of the Bible. For me, nothing in Scripture other than the life (and death) of Christ has offered a more profound challenge to my leadership style.

The setting is the garden of Eden. Creation is completed, authority has been given, and Adam and Eve have at their disposal and command the entire created order of earth. Then Eve is tempted by Satan and sins. Tragedy! But it is the surrounding circumstances and subsequent chain of events that I find most tragic. Where was Adam? Why did he not lead, challenge, or intervene? He was right there with her! Had he yielded to peace at any price? Did he simply believe it was Eve's choice?

And then the drama heightens. Adam is confronted by God himself. God's question, "Adam, where are you?" was not an inquiry. It was an invitation—an invitation to repentance, to responsibility, perhaps even to redemption of sorts. Now imagine Eve, tormented with guilt, shame, and sheer terror as she awaits Adam's reply. What will he say? How will he respond? Surely his love will cover her. What horror and depth of pain must have pierced her soul as she saw her husband point and say, "It was her." How she must have felt betrayed and abandoned! And so it began. Eve then blames the serpent, and the glory of marital love and trust and union is forever marred until the cross can make all things new.

The temptation here is to rise up in self-righteous indignation and condemn Adam for his treason and cowardice. And I would yield to that temptation except for the painful awareness that Adam's failure has too often been my failure. Blameshifting. Rationalizing. Avoiding the challenges of leadership, confrontation, and personal responsibility.

Men, we can look at our weaknesses and tendencies and try to see where they began. More importantly, let's now determine that those failures will come to an end! By God's all-triumphant grace we will lead and love and cover and care. We will look to Jesus, the last Adam, as our example—and source (Ro 5:14-21; 1Co 15:45-49). And we will love our wives as Christ loves the Church.

> ❝ If I were to put my finger on one devastating sin today, it would not be the so-called women's movement, but the lack of spiritual leadership by men at home and in the church...Pride and self-pity and fear and laziness and confusion are luring many men into self-protecting, self-exalting cocoons of silence. And to the degree that this makes room for women to take more leadership it is sometimes even endorsed as a virtue. But I believe that deep down the men—and the women—know better.
>
> Where are the men with a moral vision for their families, a zeal for the house of the Lord, a magnificent commitment to the advancement of the kingdom, an articulate dream for the mission of the church and a tenderhearted tenacity to make it real?[9] ❞
>
> —John Piper

Food, Shelter, and Much, Much More

Meditate on Hebrews 7:23-28. Aren't you glad your wife has someone like this working on her behalf?

When I speak of meeting the needs of our wives I am not referring to weaknesses, nor am I denying the pre-eminence of Jesus Christ as the source and supply of her deepest needs. I am saying that God's Word commands us as husbands to serve them in ways no one else can. We are unique channels of provision for our wives. In that regard, and by God's grace, it is our privilege to participate in meeting their needs.

> **"** Although it is true that our needs are fully met in Christ, it is also true that the Lord normally uses husbands and wives as his instruments to develop within each other a conscious awareness of personal worth. It is Christ alone who grants us security and significance, but it is often (by no means always) our spouses who help us to *feel* worthwhile.[10] **"**
>
> **—Larry Crabb**

Our wives' first need, of course, is for a growing and thriving relationship with the Lord. Even when we fail, God must be sufficient for them. God desires to meet their needs abundantly so that they are secure, joyful, and growing in his grace. But he has also given us an important role in their life. Here are three areas where we can help him fulfill his purpose for our wives:

Spirit. We must encourage our wives to cultivate intimacy with God—to become increasingly aware of his love, growing in their ability to hear his voice and walk by faith in his will. Our leadership begins with our example. Then we are to assist our wives in developing the spiritual disciplines of worship, prayer, Bible study, and waiting on God. We should also help them discern how God wants them to serve and exercise their spiritual gifts in the home and in the local church.

---

4 In your enthusiasm to lead, you share the following insights with your wife. You think they're from God. She's not so sure. Help her discern the source of each.

"Dear, I sense the Lord saying that you should..."

	From God	From You
Spend some more time with your friends	❏	❏
Get back in the habit of making desserts	❏	❏
Study what the Bible teaches about grace	❏	❏
Clean the bathrooms a little more frequently	❏	❏
Boost your energy levels by exercising	❏	❏
Lose 50 pounds in the next month	❏	❏

If you really want to serve your wife, pray for her. Ask God to pour out his grace and wisdom on her, as well as assure her of his presence and power on her behalf. Few things are as difficult to achieve as consistency in prayer; few things have prayer's potential for meeting your wife's deepest needs. Also, demonstrate your care by watching her schedule to make sure she's not being overwhelmed by demands.

Soul. Encourage your wife's intellectual interests. What does she like to read? Do you discuss current events? Don't treat her like your pupil, but lead her into areas that will keep her mind sharp and perceptive. Sometimes you may need to challenge her will to help her develop her full potential. Betsy used to be afraid to stand in front of people and teach. Eventually I realized that in my effort to protect her I had actually been stifling her. So I began gently challenging her, little by little, to speak out. She worked at it and made tremendous progress. To hear her speak today, and to see the impact she has on those listening, makes me so glad this talent didn't stay buried beneath her fear and my over-protection.

For Further Study:
Read how God "drafted" the reluctant Gideon in Judges 6. What would have happened to Israel if God hadn't challenged Gideon's will?

You are also responsible before God to contribute to your wife's emotional health. How? Nurture her with encouragement. Care enough to confront her when necessary. Comfort her when she is sad or discouraged. Create a secure environment where she is equally free to laugh or cry, to be busy or sit quietly, to listen or to openly express herself. Creatively and consistently cherish her as the priceless gift that she is to you. After the love of God, the unconditional love of her husband should be a wife's most treasured possession.

---

5 Does your wife show any of these signs of a possible internal struggle? Don't exaggerate the problem, but be careful you don't ignore symptoms like these.

❑ Decreased involvement in church activities

❑ Difficulty worshiping God

❑ Lack of faith that God can or will help

❑ Doubts about her own salvation

❑ Excessive dependence on church leadership

❑ Uncertainty about God's personal love

❑ Inability to serve (no interest or energy)

❑ Difficulty discussing spiritual life

Body. Compared to spiritual and emotional needs, our wives' physical needs are usually easy to recognize. Let's look at four needs in particular.

Home. It doesn't matter whether you rent or own, but your wife needs a home that is adequate, safe, and convenient. What you save on a "Handyman's Special" might not be a bargain if it costs your wife her sense of peace and security. Also, be alert to her need for relationships. Before moving into a home that is some distance away from her friends, family, or the life of the church, consider the long-term impact it will have on her. She may opt for less space and a smaller home in order to keep her relationships intact.

> 66 For the man who appreciates the willingness of his wife to stand against the tide of public opinion—staying at home in her empty neighborhood in the exclusive company of jelly-faced toddlers and strong willed adolescents—it is about time you gave her some help. I'm not merely suggesting that you wash the dishes or sweep the floor. I'm referring to the provision of emotional support...of conversation...of making her feel like a lady...of building her ego...of giving her one day of recreation each week...of taking her out to dinner...of telling her that you love her. Without these armaments, she is left defenseless against the foes of the family—the foes of *your* family![11] 99
>
> —**James Dobson**

Clothing. You'll be happy to know Scripture doesn't require outfitting your wife in cosmopolitan style. But we should see to it that our wives have an adequate, contemporary wardrobe. Not necessarily expensive or high fashion, but outfits which embellish the natural beauty God has given them.

Food and exercise. Your wife's health and even her emotions can be dramatically affected by her diet and exercise. Does she have enough in the food budget to meet your family's nutritional needs? When you play basketball with the guys or work out at the gym, do you provide similar opportunities for her to have fun and keep herself in shape?

Sex. This is to be every bit as enjoyable and fulfilling for our wives as it is for us. If we are willing, we can lead them into a very satisfying sexual relationship.

Seriously, Paul...

Although we mentioned this passage earlier, reread Ephesians 5:25-33. Meditate on it. Ponder its awesome implications. If I weren't convinced the Bible is God's Word, Paul's command would seem totally unreasonable and more than a bit radical: "Husbands, love your wives, just as Christ loved the church." Did he have any idea what he was asking?

Meditate on 2 Corinthians 3:4-6. Are you qualified to love your wife the way Christ loves the church? These three verses will annihilate pride and boost your faith!

God did, and he is the One standing behind this command. That this is even a possibility staggers my imagination. Me? Love Betsy as Christ loves me? Doesn't God know how selfish I can be? Of course—but he wouldn't give the command if it couldn't be carried out. This is probably the highest call that can be placed upon a man, yet God makes us adequate. Through him all things—even this—are possible.

Here's what it means to love your wife as Christ loves the Church:

Love her unconditionally and not on the basis of performance. You can't expect to keep your emotions at fever pitch, but you can commit yourself to loving her at all times. That's a decision. Determine now that you are going to love this woman as she has never been loved and never will be loved by anyone else as long as she lives. With that commitment in place your love will continue to grow and deepen, both in sickness and health, conflict and peace, sorrow and joy, failure and success, and need and abundance. Every year you will become more grateful for this woman God has given you.

---

6 Write down two or three things your wife does which really bother you.

-
-
-

Be honest: Do these affect your love for her? If she never changed in these areas, would you still be able to love her wholeheartedly?

Love her ceaselessly. Your decision to love unconditionally should be matched by corresponding action. What response would your wife give if someone asked, "How do you know your husband loves you?" It's a fair question. She should be able to point to creative and consistent expressions of your love.

For Further Study: Are you serving your wife with the attitude and to the extent Paul served the churches? (See Php 2:17; 2Co 12:15)

Love her sacrificially. True love is costly. You may be forced to make painful sacrifices in order to uphold the covenant of marriage. Loving your wife will require you to lay down your life for the rest of your life. Each day ask yourself, "What am I doing for my wife that involves personal sacrifice?" What am I doing for my wife today that costs me something? David defined sacrifice as offering the Lord that which cost him something (2Sa 24:24).

Give her yourself, not just your gifts. Of all the gifts God has given the Church, none is as precious as Jesus himself. He give all that he has *and* all that he is. We should imitate his example. Our wives appreciate gifts, but what they desire most is us.

Pour yourself out in a way that transforms her. In Ephesians 5 Paul says Jesus will present his bride (the Church) without stain, wrinkle, or blemish. That radical transformation does not come effortlessly. Our Lord made the ultimate investment, spilling out his blood so the Church could be cleansed and purified.

> 66 Love actually encompasses two dimensions. There is the dimension of *being in love* (emotional) and there is the dimension of *behaving in love* (behavioral). These are two distinctly different entities. And whereas the world tends to endorse the first of these two dimensions as its perspective of what love is, Christendom advances a view which includes them both.[12] 99
>
> **—Donald R. Harvey**

I believe we also will have the privilege of presenting our wife to God. We obviously lack Christ's transforming power, but we should have a desire to see her being continually transformed into a beautiful, spotless bride. I hope one day to be able to say, "Father, here's your daughter. It's been my privilege to love and serve her, and by your grace I've been a good steward of this wonderful gift. Now I give her back to you."

I'm not trying to make my marriage a perpetual honeymoon. What I do seek to maintain, however, is the anticipation, joy, and fulfillment we experienced during that season. I want to spend my life loving Betsy thoroughly and completely. When the day comes for me to present her to God, I trust she will reflect these years of investment.

Love her without bitterness. The closer you are to someone, the greater his or her potential to hurt you. Your wife will inevitably cause you pain. When that happens, forgive her as Christ forgave you, and don't let yourself become embittered (Col 3:19).

Love her as you love your own body. If we did this, our wives would never again question the extent of our love.

"After all," wrote Paul, "no one ever hated his own body, but he feeds it and cares for it, just as Christ does the church" (Eph 5:29). Hate our bodies? Not exactly! We pamper ourselves, nursing little pains and satisfying certain appetites and desires. Our wives would be in good shape if we gave them half the attention we give ourselves.

Give her something worth reflecting. This idea comes from the verse that says "[man] is the image and glory of God; but the woman is the glory of man" (1Co 11:7). In other words, your wife is a reflection of you.

Pause for a moment to let that sink in, and I think you'll find it sobering. When people look into the mirror of your wife's life, do you know what they see? You. Your investment. When she is not doing well, there's good reason to question your care for her.

You shouldn't take this too far; your wife is responsible for maintaining her relationship with God, and her obedience doesn't depend on you. If she is healthy and alive with the life of God, that is first and foremost a testimony to her walk with Christ. But the condition of her spirit, soul, and body reflects the investment you have made in your relationship. If you want her to be your glory, make sure she has something glorious to reflect.

Cherish her as your precious possession. I enjoy exploring used book stores and collecting old books. Can you guess how I'd react if someone set his coffee mug on my 1866 edition of J.G. Holland's *Life of Abraham Lincoln*? Actually, I'd never give him the opportunity—I keep it in a very safe place. And yet without even thinking about it, I can injure my most priceless earthly treasure— my wife Betsy—with a careless remark or neglect.

Would you leave the windows of your new car down during a rainstorm? Would you let your child drink grape juice in the living room just after getting new carpet installed? Definitely not. So why aren't we as passionately protective when something happens to our wives or, worse yet, when we do something to them ourselves? I want to be more enthusiastic about Betsy than I am about anything else God has given me. I want to meditate on her potential and frequently remind her of how important she is to me. I want to jealously guard her, treating her tenderly as a precious gift.

Men, most of us know what it's like to set goals. We know how to identify a task—whether it's building a house, finishing a report, or earning a degree—and then take certain steps to complete it. In principle, loving our wives is no different.

Meditate on Matthew 6:21. Though not a reference to marriage, here's a principle that will add lots to your relationship with your wife.

Marriage can seem like an overwhelming task if you're trying to follow biblical standards. Yet we face this task by the grace of God, empowered by the Holy Spirit, guided by the teaching of Scripture, and—as members of an authentic local church—supported by other men with similar resolve. We *can* do it. Make the decision to love your wife. Act on the things you've been learning in this book. And if you feel overwhelmed or completely inadequate, lean on the One whose love for you has always been more than adequate—even when it led him to the cross. ■

GROUP DISCUSSION These questions will probably be most effective if wives are not present for the discussion. Share honestly, but remember to share in a way that honors your spouse.

❱ What do you find most difficult to understand about your wife?

❱ How well do you control your temper during conflict?

❱ Some husbands are overbearing dictators, some are compromising diplomats. What's your leadership style?

❱ How do you show honor to your wife?

❱ Do you have any trouble agreeing with the biblical statement that "the head of the woman is man"? Explain.

❱ What are your wife's main responsibilities in the home?

❱ How often do you pray for your wife?

❱ What are the two biggest challenges your wife is facing at this time?

❱ Is your wife a good reflection on you?

❱ How could you lead more effectively in your home?

Answer to Warm-Up
(from page 67): D. Dan Marino and Mark Clayton. Marino's 5,084 yards remains an NFL record. But without Clayton's reliable hands, he never could have succeeded. Just as quarterback and receiver must cooperate to move the ball down field, so must a husband and wife work together in mutual submission to make a marriage successful. (This illustration is adapted from *Point Man* by Steve Farrar, pp. 163–64.)

RECOMMENDED READING *Recovering Biblical Manhood and Womanhood* by John Piper and Wayne Grudem, eds. (Wheaton, IL: Crossway Books, © 1991)

Point Man by Steve Farrar (Portland, OR: Multnomah Press, © 1990)

THE UNLIMITED WORTH OF A WIFE

BETSY RICUCCI

SCRIPTURE TEXT Titus 2:3-5

WARM-UP If someone offered you your weight in jewels, which of the following would have the greatest value?

A. Emeralds

B. Rubies

C. Diamonds

D. Sapphires

E. Amethysts

(See page 101 for answer)

PERSONAL STUDY Just hearing the word "role" can make some women bristle. It sounds restrictive—at least that's what today's culture would argue. In virtually every ad, movie, and TV show women are being taught, "Why should anyone place boundaries around you? You can be anything you want."

But think for a moment about a river. A river without a boundary is nothing but a swamp. What does a swamp produce? Things like mosquitoes and disease. Where there are boundaries, though, there is *action*. There is *current*. There is *direction*. And there is *purpose*.

There *are* boundaries surrounding the role of a wife. We have a unique position in life, and I think you'll be encouraged and inspired as you see the value of it. In order for that role to have meaning, though, it's necessary that we understand it—and understand the forces attacking it.

The divorce rate in America is now higher than in any other civilized nation in the world. In this century alone, it has increased 700%. That number is incomprehensible

Meditate on Proverbs 29:18. Do you think this verse explains our culture's push for "women's liberation"?

to me. And the last time the White House appointed a conference on families, they didn't even know what a "family" was. All this confusion and chaos makes it increasingly difficult for the Christian woman to get her bearings. Connie Marshner, a wife, mother, and author, describes her own struggles:

"I had learned at my mother's knee that the only things that matter were the achievements and rewards of the world—that a woman shouldn't have to depend on a man for anything, that life wasn't worth anything if you didn't control your own destiny, and that children were slavery. Does it seem contradictory that I was defending traditional values on the public stage and living such a non-traditional life? It shouldn't. I was defending traditional values out of a deeply held intellectual conviction. But I was living my life out of a deeply held emotional disposition. I still hold the intellectual conviction—it was correct to begin with. But through the grace of God the emotional disposition is being healed.

"Maybe you didn't get the feminist preaching from your mother. Maybe you got it at school instead. But it has some attractiveness, doesn't it? It makes you feel important, and you deserve more than a life of mere domesticity. Right? Don't think that just because you're a believing Christian you're immune to the lure of feminism. What your mind believes, and what your emotions dictate can be two very different things, and you might not realize the contradiction."[1]

> **❝** The life which is unexamined is not worth living. **❞**
>
> —**Plato**

How can we know whether feminism and the other cultural pressures which bombard us daily have affected our outlook? The best place to start is by examining our values. Evaluation is hard, and it can be painful to see where you really are. Yet if we desire the benefits of change, let's muster the courage to ask ourselves, "Are my values biblical or are they any different than the values of this culture?"

1 Who is the one woman in the world (living or dead) you would most like to resemble?

Three Things The World Values Most

Our society is preoccupied with the *present*. We want to buy it all now, have it all now, experience it all now. We're dissatisfied with anything less than instant gratification. It's a perfectly logical response, when you think about it. Evolutionary theory has robbed humanity of its sense of long-term purpose. Since (theoretically) we came from nothing and are going into nothing, all we have is now. We might as well make the most of it. This explains why our culture places such emphasis on the present.

Our culture also worships *individuality*. Americans are in love with independence. Since July 4, 1776, this has been our national characteristic. However, the independence of today is a far cry from the noble goal of winning our freedom from tyrannical rule. Today we want freedom from *all* rules or *any* restrictions that would hinder our individual expression. This type of independence produces some unattractive and unhealthy fruit, including isolation, competition, and pride. I once read of a town with houses that had yards the size of a postage stamp, and yet everyone had their own lawnmowers. They were too independent to borrow from anybody else!

In the last century, this national spirit of independence has led to a breakdown in relationships. The commitment to marriage has eroded. Friendships among women have suffered as well. We view one another more as competitors than comrades and allies. We go to the local shopping mall and get sucked into the comparison game: What are other women wearing? Which hairstyles are most flattering? Who has the most advanced stroller? And unless we come out on top in every category, we can easily struggle with envy.

For Further Study: To see what Solomon concluded from his uninhibited pursuit of pleasure, read Ecclesiastes 2:1-11; 12:1-7.

Achievement and accomplishment form the third leg of our cultural philosophy. It has been said that 80 percent of America's adult population is on a search for self-fulfillment. We devote so much energy to enhancing our beauty, extending our education, furthering our career, and acquiring material possessions. Yet satisfying our selfish desires is like trying to fill up a bottomless pit; its appetite is insatiable.

It is virtually impossible not to be affected by a society where selfish views predominate. I am a wife, mother, and homemaker—not a doctor or corporate executive. I can reach the end of a day and think, *What have I accomplished today that was really worthwhile? No brain surgeries, no multi-million dollar profits...Well, I scrubbed the floor, read to the children, and made a meal for a sick neighbor.* It is so easy to feel my work has no value. But we need to evaluate what is important. Are we living for eternal or temporal values? Keeping those questions in mind will help keep us on track to fulfill God's purpose.

R.C. Sproul says that how we live our life reveals our deepest convictions about life. Take a hard look at your values. Ask your friends what they see as the driving motive in your life. And periodically ask yourself questions along these lines:

■ Who has shaped my view of being a wife?

■ Would my husband feel he is the most important person in my life? Why or why not?

■ What am I doing, why am I doing it, and who am I doing it for?

> ❝ Women today are under tremendous pressure to be successful. They have been told they can establish high-power careers, raise ideal children, be ravishing wives, and in their spare time keep physically fit, pursue outside interests, and develop an independent financial strategy. Women who think they can have it all have bought into a cruel illusion. They cannot have it all. They cannot do it all. No one can…More than ever, women must be encouraged to carefully examine their values. Values determine choices. And women's choices have never been more critical. The world values what is tangible and visible. God values the invisible and eternal. Immediate satisfaction is a grave enemy to living by godly values. I realize that if I lived for what made me feel good at the end of each day, I would live for all the wrong things.[2] ❞
>
> —**Jean Fleming**

A Tale of Two Women

Scripture gives us God's point of view—the only opinion that counts—on the role of the wife. You won't find a simpler or more comprehensive definition than that given in Proverbs 14:1: "The wise woman builds her house, but with her own hands the foolish one tears hers down." There's no confusion about this definition. We're either wise or foolish. We're either building our families or tearing them apart.

The Hebrew verb translated as "builds" in this verse encompasses a vast range of meaning. It can refer to construction and heavy labor; it can involve fashioning and creating things; it can also speak of fortifying or restoring. The wise wife does all of these in marriage. She exerts tremendous effort. But the foolish womans tears down and overthrows her house. Proud and arrogant, she seeks the best for herself at the expense of her marriage.

Meditate on Colossians 3:1-6. How often do you think the dead worry about self-fulfillment?

We get a more detailed picture of the wise wife when Paul shares this pastoral advice with Titus:

> Likewise, teach the older women to be reverent in the way they live, not to be slanderers or addicted to much wine, but to teach what is good. Then they can train the younger women to love their husbands and children, to be self-controlled and pure, to be busy at home, to be kind, and to be subject to their husbands, so that no one will malign the word of God (Tit 2:3-5).

The last part of that verse has gripped me. How do we malign and discredit the word of God? By saying things like, "Oh come on—those verses were written centuries ago in another culture. They certainly don't apply to us today. That's just not reality."

For Further Study:
Two of the main biblical passages which discuss roles in marriage are found in 1 Corinthians 11:3-12 and 1 Timothy 2:11-15.

God's Word is as applicable now as it was when it was first written. It's authority over our lives has not changed. Paul's counsel to Titus doesn't reflect first-century culture—it reflects the order God established in creation. Eve was made to be subject to Adam. I was made to be subject to my husband Gary. No matter what happens in our culture or how unpopular the biblical definition becomes, our God-given role remains the same.

One glimpse at the relationships our culture has produced should be enough to drive us right back to Titus 2. Selfish independence and instant gratification don't work! It's a tragic mirage. True fulfillment comes by yielding our lives to the biblical pattern. Better yet, we have the unsurpassed joy of bringing honor to God through our obedience to his commands.

When I said to Gary, "I will," I accepted God's call to be a wife. I don't "do" a wife, I *am* a wife. Fulfilling my call as a wife is the platform for everything else I do. My actions, my interests, and my activities will all be assessed in light of this call to build my house wisely.

---

2 *Self* magazine asked its readers if they would ever consider having an extramarital affair even if no one would find out. Can you guess what percentage said they *would not* consider an affair? (Answer printed upside down at bottom of next page.)

Women   **Men**

89

Are you familiar with the story about Mary anointing Jesus with costly perfume (Mk 14:3-9)? It's one of my favorites, though the act didn't sit well with those who were watching. "Why this waste of perfume?" they muttered. "It could have been sold for more than a year's wages and the money given to the poor." Jesus interpreted her gesture in a different light: "She has done a beautiful thing for me...wherever the gospel is preached throughout the world, what she has done will also be told, in memory of her" (v.6,9).

Some say you're wasting your gifts and talents as a wife. Not Jesus. The value he places on your servanthood goes far beyond what money or status could ever achieve.

Who Wields The Power?

You may be surprised that I haven't yet mentioned the superhuman woman described in Proverbs 31 who buys fields, plants vineyards, feeds the poor, clothes her household, and a dozen other things—all with a perfect attitude. Have you ever turned to that passage of Scripture seeking inspiration and come away feeling like you don't measure up?

Scripture doesn't include this section in order to condemn us, but to reveal the vast potential we have as women. This is no unfulfilled, one-dimensional wife. She is incredibly competent, resourceful, and creative. Her opportunities to make a lasting impact on others are unlimited. So are ours. But pay close attention to the goal of this wife's service. Is she working for personal gain? No—in all she does, she lives to benefit those around her.

God has given women a tremendous capacity for unique and worthwhile accomplishment, and he calls us to use it in service to others. First on the list should be our husbands. Here's where we can prove the truth of Jesus' words: "The greatest among you will be your servant" (Mt 23:11).

Our Lord's statement has more significance than you may realize. In a kingdom, who has more power—the king or his advisor? One has the power of position; one has the power of influence. The advisor is obviously the

> **❝** Where men are to rule the direction of life, women are to rule its quality. Whereas men provide leadership, women provide atmosphere. Whereas men control the choices, women control the environment.[3] **❞**
>
> —Jean Brand

king's servant, yet history shows time and again what an immense impact a trusted counselor can make. It's much the same with marriage. While the husband holds the power of position, his wife retains the tremendous power of influence.

Consider Queen Esther's clout with King Xerxes. Jews throughout the vast Persian empire were saved from extermination by her gentle persuasion. And though her goals were far less noble, Jezebel had a dramatic effect on the nation of Israel during her husband's reign. Scripture is so poignant: "Surely there was no one like Ahab who sold himself to do evil in the sight of the Lord, because Jezebel his wife incited him" (IKi 21:25 NAS).

For Further Study: In Ephesians 5 and 1 Peter 3, Scripture addresses the woman first and then the man. What does that tell you about a wife's power of influence?

The power of influence works behind the scenes. Most of us would probably prefer the spotlight. I believe that's why so many women in our culture compete with their husbands for power. They greatly underestimate their own potential. In grasping for the power of position, however, they forfeit the power of influence.

Don't compete with your husband. Serve and counsel him. If you grab for *his* position, you will only succeed in losing *your* influence.

This is a bit of a tangent, but I've spoken to many women who question whether it's right for a wife to work outside the home. Does she undermine her husband's leadership by taking a job? Could it be perceived as competition? Is her employment a hindrance or a help in serving her husband?

If a couple has no children or if the children are grown, the answer depends primarily on one's motive and values. The following exercise will help you ask the right kinds of questions to determine that. On the other hand, if young children are involved, the questions take a different spin. The lure of a career, the desire to maintain a certain lifestyle, ignorance of the vast opportunities to make a meaningful contribution from the home...all these can rob a woman of the ultimate satisfaction of raising her own children. Especially during the pre-school years, when a mother's care and influence are so vital.

> 66 There is...cause for concern—major concern—when young couples make their primary commitment to their careers, and then choose to have children "on the side" ...This may detonate a few land mines, but parents, I have to remind you that nannies, baby-sitters, relatives, and day-care workers will never give an ultimate account to God for how they raised your children. You will give that account. You will.[4] 99
>
> —Bill Hybels

I am convinced God will honor the wife and husband who make their children a higher priority than their lifestyle or leisure. For those of you who are single mothers and have to work to support your family, I so respect you and trust God for a unique grace upon you and your children. May he establish you in a local church that provides the kind of care and support you need to fulfill the high call of motherhood.

---

3 If applicable, use the following questions to help evaluate whether you should consider employment outside the home.

Is my interest in employment motivated by...

	Yes	No
■ Financial need?	❑	❑
■ Sense of accomplishment or value?	❑	❑
■ Personal security?	❑	❑

Are the benefits of outside work greater than its costs to my...

	Yes	No
■ Personal life?	❑	❑
■ Spiritual, emotional, and physical health?	❑	❑
■ Marriage?	❑	❑
■ Children?	❑	❑
■ Other relationships?	❑	❑
■ Church involvement?	❑	❑

As you examine your values, you can gain the proper motivation to do whatever it is God has called you to do. Remember, though, that our efforts have the greatest value when they benefit other people, and especially those people closest to us.

What Your Husband Really Needs

I can probably assume that you've read the previous study describing your husband's role. That's fair—he will no doubt be flipping through this one as well! As long as you leave God in charge of your spouse's response, it helps to know what the other is working toward. If you haven't read Study 5 yet, let me assure you: Gary laid it on the line. Your husband has his work cut out for him.

But now it's our turn. We're no less responsible for the condition of our marriage. I want to challenge us to do everything we can to succeed as wives. Being a wife is a tremendous responsibility and an awesome privilege. And to a large degree, our success will rest on our ability to cultivate the following four attitudes.

Respect. The Bible doesn't mince any words on this topic: "Let the wife see to it that she respect her husband" (Eph 5:33 NAS). Initially we find it easy to obey this command. We marry Sir Hubby convinced he is our knight in shining armor. What a wonderful man! But within a few years...or months...or hours, the cracks begin to appear. His faults start to surface. Suddenly the picture isn't so rosy anymore and we think, "I'm supposed to respect *that?* If he wants my respect, let him earn it."

Meditate on 1 Peter 3:1-4. Does this redefine your understanding of beauty?

Look again at Ephesians 5:33—you won't find any conditions your husband must meet before he deserves your respect. Scripture does not authorize you to say, "Do X, Y, and Z and then maybe I will respect you." You're commanded to respect him simply because he is your husband. Be careful not to use a double standard. You want him to accept you the way you are, don't you? At times it will be difficult, but you need to give him the same level of acceptance and respect.

We show our respect through our thoughts, words, and deeds. If you tend to see his faults more than his strengths, start looking for things in his life that are praiseworthy. Does he keep a steady job? That's something to respect! Both of you will benefit by your saying, "You know, I really respect the fact that day in and day out you get up and go to work." You may have to start small, but start somewhere.

> **❝** If you treat a man as he is, he will stay as he is. But if you treat him as if he were what he ought to be and could be, he will become the bigger and better man. **❞**
>
> **—Goethe**

Respect acts as a bridge between you and your husband. It makes him open to receiving from you, even in cases where you need to share something corrective. If you are respecting him and manifesting your esteem, it will be easy for you to drive the truth of your concerns over that bridge. But if you're disrespectful, you're destroying a vital avenue you have to communicate your concerns, wishes, and desires. Every expression of respect will make that bridge stronger and better able to support your communication.

Gratitude. When you think of your husband, do you think of all he does to provide, lead, and care for you and your family? Or do you think of all he *should* do but doesn't? Perhaps you have stewed over thoughts like, *He's supposed to do that. That's part of the marriage contract! He knew the job was dangerous when he took it.*

Nothing destroys gratitude more quickly than expectation. If you think your husband owes you things, you may mentally and emotionally lock him up in a sort of "debtor's prison" until he pays what is due. It's hard to be a debtor. Unless you want him to treat you the same way, do not imprison your husband with expectations. Instead, cultivate and express a genuine appreciation for him. Husbands will respond much more quickly to our gratitude than to our griping. When disappointed expectations begin to affect you, encourage yourself the way David did: "Find rest, O my soul, in God alone; my hope comes from him" (Ps 62:5).

Meditate on Philippians 4:6-7.
What's the best outlet for frustration?

Your husband's self-image is directly connected to your public and private admiration and praise. Look for unique ways to say, "I really love being your wife." By creatively expressing your gratitude for your husband, you are first of all obeying God. You are also protecting your marriage from the disappointment, criticism, and complaining that can creep in through the door of selfishness and ungratefulness.

---

4 Some time this week, express your gratitude for your husband in a way you never have before. Use the following ideas to get your creativity rolling!

- Send him a card
- Deliver a helium balloon to his office
- Give him a gift
- Give him a back rub

- Plan a surprise date
- Buy a sexy nightgown
- Write him a poem
- Other _____

Shortly after I was married, a wise friend told me, "Unhappiness is a public rebuke to your husband." I've thought about that many times since. I know God doesn't want us to be dishonest and hide our emotions under a perma-grin. But if we are continually unhappy, we need to seek the Lord for a solution. And invariably, ladies, that solution begins with God changing us, not us changing our husbands!

Servant's heart. Having a servant's heart simply means you are excited to make others successful. The best test of your servanthood is at home! Why? Because no one is there giving you a standing ovation for doing seven loads of laundry. No matter how much you sweat over the stove or how many dishes you wash, you can't expect a fat bonus or a company award. You serve day in and day out with little or no recognition. Even Jesus went through this. You would think his neighbors would have been most receptive to his ministry, having known and observed him for years. But they resisted him more than anyone, causing Jesus to remark, "Only in his hometown and in his own house is a prophet without honor" (Mt 13:57). Serving at home will purge your motives of any selfish ambition and teach you to focus on the interests of others.

> **❝** If we fully comprehended the brevity of life, our greatest desire would be to serve one another. Instead, the illusion of permanence leads us to scrap and claw for power and demand the best for ourselves.[5] **❞**
>
> **—James Dobson**

When Jesus was baptized, his Father said, "This is my Son, whom I love; with him I am well pleased" (Mt 3:17). What had Jesus done to receive such praise? Nothing but live in his own home, honoring his parents and serving in his father's carpentry business. Apparently that was enough to please God.

All four Gospels say those who want to save their life will lose it, but those who lose their life will find it. That's servanthood. Let's put the identity crisis to rest right there. Servanthood is where we are going to find life.

Trust. The American Heritage Dictionary defines trust as "Confidence in the integrity, ability, character, and truth of a person or thing." In order to trust our husbands, however, we must first be confident in the integrity, ability, character, and truth of God. Unless we trust God, we won't have the grace necessary to trust our husbands.

This brings us right to the biblical principle of submission. Oh, the assault this principle has been subjected to in the last few decades! But as I see it, such ridicule and resistance only highlights the importance and impact of submission if properly understood and obeyed.

In the book *Recovering Biblical Manhood and Womanhood,* John Piper succinctly defines submission as a *"disposition* to yield to the husband's authority and an *inclination* to follow his leadership."[6] The book devotes an entire chapter to the passage in 1 Peter which begins, "Wives, in the same way be submissive to your husbands..." (1Pe 3:1). Because there is so much confusion and misunderstanding regarding the nature and practice of submission, let me quote at length from Wayne Grudem's extended definition:

Submission is an inner quality of gentleness that affirms the leadership of the husband. "Be submissive to your husbands" means that a wife will willingly submit to her husband's authority and leadership in the marriage. It means making a choice to affirm her husband as leader within the limits of obedience to Christ. It includes a demeanor that honors him as leader even when she dissents. Of course, it is an attitude that goes much deeper than mere obedience, but the idea of willing obedience to a husband's authority is certainly part of this submission...

Further understanding of the nature of this submission is gained from Peter's description of the beauty that accompanies it, the beauty of "a gentle and quiet spirit, which is of great worth in God's sight" (verse 4). The adjective *gentle*... means "not insistent on one's own rights," or "not pushy, not selfishly assertive," "not demanding one's own way." Such a gentle and quiet spirit will be beautiful before other human beings, even unbelieving husbands (verses 1-2), but even more important, it "is of great worth in God's sight." Why? No doubt because such a spirit is the result of quiet and continual trust in God to supply one's needs, and God delights in being trusted (cf. 1 Peter 1:5, 7-9, 21; 2:6-7, 23; 5:7)...

Submission involves obedience like Sarah's. Quiet confidence in God produces in a woman the imperishable beauty of a gentle and quiet spirit, but it also enables her to submit to her husband's authority without fear that it will ultimately be harmful to her well-being or personhood.

Peter uses Sarah's submission to Abraham as an example of such submissiveness to a husband. Wives are to be submissive to their husbands (verse 5) as Sarah obeyed Abraham, calling him her master (or "lord"). Peter does not seem to be referring to any one specific incident here, for the main verb and both participles in verse 5 all indicate a continuing pattern of conduct during one's life...

The example of Sarah's obedience would be an appropriate encouragement to the wives to whom Peter was writing, for Sarah became the mother of all God's people

Meditate on Proverbs 3:5-6. Are you willing to lean on God's understanding rather than your own?

in the old covenant (Isa 51:2; cf. Gal 4:22-26), even though there had been many times in which following Abraham had meant trusting God in uncertain, unpleasant, and even dangerous situations (Ge 12:1, 5, 10-15; 13:1; 20:2-6 [cf. verse 12]; 22:3). Yet Peter says believing women are now her children (or "daughters"), the true members of her spiritual family. To be Sarah's daughter is to be a joint heir of the promises and the honor given to her and to Abraham.

The condition for being Sarah's "daughters" is "if you do what is right and do not give way to fear" (verse 6)... Peter's insistence on doing what is right is a reminder that no acts of disobedience in Sarah's life are to be imitated by Christian wives (cf. Ge 16:2, 6; 18:15; perhaps 20:5); it is her submission to her husband and her trust in God that Peter commends. The condition "if you...do not give way to fear" is another way in which faith finds expression. A woman with a gentle and quiet spirit who continues hoping in God will not be terrified by circumstances or by an unbelieving or disobedient husband (cf. Ge 20:6)...

Submission acknowledges an authority that is not totally mutual. Although Peter is speaking specifically to wives in this section, many people today object to any kind of submission that is required of wives and not of husbands. In order to avoid the force of any command that would tell wives to be submissive to their husbands' authority, evangelical feminists frequently talk about "mutual submission" within marriage. The phrase itself is slippery, because it can mean different things. On the one hand, it can mean simply that husbands and wives are to be thoughtful and considerate toward one another and put each other's interests and preferences before their own. If people use the phrase to apply to such *mutual*

SUBMISSION DOES *NOT* MEAN...

■ Putting a husband in the place of Christ.

■ Giving up independent thought.

■ A wife should give up efforts to influence and guide her husband.

■ A wife should give in to every demand of her husband. *If he should say, "Stop being a Christian, be like me," she will have to humbly say, "I cannot. My conscience must answer to a higher authority." If he should tell her to steal, or lie, or do something else contrary to the clear moral teachings of Scripture, she must refuse.*

■ A wife has lesser intelligence or competence.

■ Being fearful or timid.

■ A wife and husband are unequal in Christ. *The command to wives to be subject to their husbands should never be taken to imply inferior personhood or spirituality, or lesser importance.*[7]

—Wayne Grudem

consideration and deference, then they are speaking of an idea that is fully consistent with the teachings of the New Testament and that still allows for a unique leadership role for the husband and a unique responsibility for the wife to submit to his authority or leadership. "Mutual submission" would then mean that the husband is to be unselfish in his exercise of leadership in the family and the wife is to be unselfish in her submission to and support of that leadership.

Although we might think that this is using the word *submission* in a rather unusual way, we would probably agree that this is a possible sense of "mutual submission." We would then say that there is "mutual submission" in some senses in marriage, but not in *all* senses, because the wife still has to submit to her husband's authority and leadership in a way that the husband does not have to—indeed, *should not*—submit to his wife's authority or leadership. He has a unique leadership role in the family that he should not abdicate...

Within a healthy Christian marriage, there will be large elements of mutual consultation and seeking of wisdom, and most decisions will come by consensus between husband and wife. For a wife to be submissive to her husband will probably not often involve obeying actual commands or directives (though it will sometimes include this), for a husband may rather give requests and seek advice and discussion about the course of action to be followed (cf. 2Co 8:8; Phil 8-9). Nevertheless, a wife's attitude of submission to her husband's authority will be reflected in numerous words and actions each day that reflect deference to his leadership and acknowledgement of his final responsibility—after discussion, whenever possible—to make decisions affecting the whole family.[9]

> 66 When a wife submits to her husband as unto the Lord, she is not destroying or subverting her authority in the home, she is establishing it. When a woman tries to undermine her husband's position in order to become "boss" of the family, she is cutting off her own strength and weakening her position in the home. Children who know that their mother is being backed up by their father, quickly respond to the order of things, and they begin to develop strength, stability, and confidence in their own lives.[8] 99
> —Roy Lessin

Dr. Grudem's style is quite a bit more formal than mine, but I trust you can appreciate the biblical truth he articulates. Ladies, we should be so grateful for godly leadership! God did not establish it to hinder, dominate, or restrict us. As a matter of fact our own authority is *strengthened*, not undermined, by submitting to the authority of our husbands. You cannot use authority properly unless you know what it's like to be under authority. The Roman centurion amazed Jesus with his reliance on this principle (Lk 7:6-9). My authority to pray, influence, train my children, and fulfill any responsibility is tremendously strengthened by my response to Gary's leadership, or greatly weakened by my resistance to his authority.

Let me ask a question that has convicted me more than once: Do you spend more time questioning, doubting, and disagreeing with your husband's direction *or* praying for him to hear God? We need to give them room to fail. That will be tough until we learn to see the value in failure. God's long-range plans are going to be accomplished despite your husband's mistakes. Who could have made a bigger mistake than Pontius Pilate when he decided to crucify the Son of God? His wife even warned him beforehand: "Don't have anything to do with that innocent man, for I have suffered a great deal today in a dream because of him" (Mt 27:19). She was right. He ignored her. Yet his failure was used to accomplish God's ultimate purpose.

For Further Study: If you feel genuinely threatened by your husband's leadership (or lack thereof), nurture your faith in God's sovereignty by studying 1 Peter 2:19-23 and Psalm 138:8.

Despite some pretty harrowing experiences, Sarah remained confident that God was in control. We can entrust to God all our concerns for our marriage and family. As Paul assured the believers in Thessalonica, "Faithful is He who calls you, and He also will bring it to pass" (1Th 5:24 NAS). To paraphrase Welsh church leader Bryn Jones, "Don't you think God is sovereign enough to swallow up all your mistakes to the greater purpose of his will?" I'm not condoning irresponsibility, but I am reminding us that because of God's sovereignty, *all things* will work together for good to those who love him.

---

5 In the space below, ask yourself (and answer) the following question: *Is there anything I do which hinders my husband from taking active leadership in our home?* Ask your husband for his response as well.

Glory or Rot?

I've read various magazine articles which attempt to estimate a homemaker's worth, ranging from $14,000 to $50,000 annually. The Bible gives its own estimate: "An excellent wife, who can find? For her worth is far above jewels" (Pr 31:10 NAS). Note here that it says excellent, not *perfect*. Your value to your husband is beyond calculation. You need this biblical assurance of your own value if you hope to withstand the cultural pressures of the day.

At his wife's funeral, the Reverend E.V. Hill shared some personal memories of their years together. He described a night when he came home and found the entire house lit up with candles. It looked very romantic. When he tried to turn on the light switch, though, nothing happened. The electricity had been shut off because they hadn't been able to afford that month's bill. Instead of screaming at him for the inconvenience, his wife had set out candles. She didn't want him to feel bad about their financial difficulty. E.V. Hill's ministry wasn't always welcome, and he recounted a time when people in the community were making bomb threats. One morning he woke up early and found his wife had gone with the car. When she returned, he asked what she had been doing. "I didn't know if there was going to be a bomb under the car," she said, "and I wanted to test it out first."

"An excellent wife is the crown of her husband, but she who shames him is as rottenness in his bones" (Pr 12:4 NAS). While reading that verse one day, I got a picture in my mind's eye of a crown. It was beautiful to look at but it wasn't being worn. And a crown only has significance when it is worn. When I am fulfilling my call as a wife I designate my husband as someone worthy of respect. That's what I want to do. I want to be the kind of crown for my husband that E.V. Hill's wife was for him.

In a society that measures value by how much money you make, what kind of house you live in, and what kind of car you drive, God measures our worth by the depth of our service. If you get only one thing out of this study, let it be this. It will help you immeasurably. When you are scrubbing out the tub or heating up dinner for a husband who is late again...when your emotions are shouting, "What do I do that has any value?"...remind yourself that you are anointing the head of Jesus with service, and it is a beautiful fragrance to him. It may never be mentioned in the grocery store tabloids, but it gets front-page coverage in the tabloids that count—in heaven. ■

Meditate on Proverbs 18:22. You are a daily manifestation of God's favor toward your husband!

100

GROUP DISCUSSION

These questions will probably be most effective if husbands are not present for the discussion. Share honestly, but remember to share in a way that honors your spouse.

▶ What one thing would you like to change about society's treatment of women?

▶ What do you consider your most worthwhile accomplishment in the past two or three years?

▶ Discuss the author's statement on page 89: "Fulfilling my call as a wife is the platform for everything else I do."

▶ Briefly describe one decision your husband has made (or is currently making) in which you found it difficult to trust him.

▶ How do you feel about women working outside the home?

▶ Do you see any evidence that feminism has influenced your thinking?

▶ How is decision-making handled in your home?

▶ Which of the four attitudes described in this study comes most naturally for you? least naturally?

▶ How often do you pray for your husband?

▶ How can you more effectively support and inspire your husband to exercise leadership in the home?

▶ Has God shown you anything through this study that will require change on your part?

Answer to Warm-Up
(from page 85):B. Rubies. According to a gemologist at the New York Diamond Connection, Inc., a very fine ruby would cost $40,000.00 per karat. If one karat weighs about five grams, and there are 454 grams in a pound, use this formula to calculate your worth in fine rubies: # of pounds x 454 (grams per pound) x $8,000 (cost per gram). At this price, a 130-pound woman would be worth $472,160,000 to her husband! Isn't it great to know your value as a wife far surpasses that (Pr 31:10)?

RECOMMENDED READING   *Creative Counterpart* by Linda Dillow (Nashville, TN: Thomas Nelson Publishers, © 1986)

MUCH ADO ABOUT MONEY

GARY AND BETSY RICUCCI

SCRIPTURE TEXT Luke 16:10-11

WARM-UP If you gave ten thousand dollars *every minute,* how long would it take to pay off the U.S. national debt?

A. 1 year

B. 3 years

C. 39 years

D. 114 years

E. 207 years

F. 615 years

(See page 117 for answer)

PERSONAL STUDY In the first chapter of this study book we mentioned the seriousness of covenant. God takes marriage very seriously. He takes money seriously, too, as Jesus explains in the Gospel of Luke: "If you have not been trustworthy in handling worldly wealth, who will trust you with true riches?" (Lk 16:11). The "true riches" in question here are spiritual riches, eternal riches. According to this verse, our spending habits and our capacity for spiritual growth are directly linked in God's economy.

Derek Prince, a Bible teacher and author, goes one step further by saying that if we are not handling money properly we cannot be in the perfect will of God. For the overwhelming majority of Americans, financial problems stem not from a weak economy but from our own lack of discipline, misplaced priorities, bad habits, and unbiblical attitudes. If our finances are in disorder, our other priorities—including the relationship we have with God and with others—are almost certainly in disarray as well.

Marriage may be the first casualty of financial chaos, as one study showed. Eighty percent of the couples surveyed, who were all in the midst of divorce proceedings, listed disagreement over finances as the reason for their split. That's four out of five! You probably are not surprised. Few married couples have dodged the stress, fear, and resentment that financial decisions can cause.

When identified and understood, however, the differences which lead a couple to fight over money *can* be used to keep their finances on track. That's the premise of this study and the testimony of our own marriage. I (Gary) am more of a spender. Betsy is a saver. My tendencies can lead me either toward generosity (good) or impulsive spending (bad); Betsy's caution can cause her to be frugal (good) or fearful (bad). The natural tension between our personalities has been a real asset. I help Betsy to more thoroughly enjoy what we have, and she makes sure we still have something to enjoy!

Husbands, you will need to obey Scripture and take primary responsibility for providing the income and managing expenses. You will both need God's help, and you will need to make use of the principles and instruction you've received thus far in this book. But your finances need not be a source of ongoing tension. Instead of being the wedge that drives your marriage apart, money issues can—by the grace and wisdom of God—provide a way to deeper unity.

Meditate on 1 Corinthians 12:17-21. What if you and your spouse always perceived finances the same way? Would you trust your money to someone with two hands but no eyes?

---

1 You have just received a check for $5,000—your share of Great Aunt Ismerelda's inheritance. List the seven ways each of you would spend it. (Wait until after you have finished to compare answers.)

How Used	Amount
1.	_____
2.	_____
3.	_____
4.	_____
5.	_____
6.	_____
7.	_____

Being a Good Provider

Though Eve got her fair share of God's curse after the fall, it was to Adam that God said, "Cursed is the ground because of you; through painful toil you will eat of it all the days of your life...By the sweat of your brow you will eat your food until you return to the ground" (Ge 3:17,19). Shirking one's duties in the name of "women's rights" is simply not an option for the Christian man. He's not honoring his reluctant wife by shoving her into the workforce. He needs to resist this cultural convenience and fulfill his sacred obligation to provide for his family. Also, he should be careful not to make personal fulfillment a prerequisite. God didn't place much emphasis on career satisfaction when pronouncing this judgment!

Before having children or after the children are grown, many couples choose to have the wife work. That second income may be an excellent way to pay off debts or build savings, assuming it doesn't take too heavy a toll on the family. Because God gives men the responsibility for provision, though, this study will be primarily addressed to husbands.

> **"** Few families are free of anxieties and contentions in the matter of family finances. To some, it is a matter of such major importance as to be an ever-festering sore, never healing and continually thwarting the happiness of the home. As a factor in marital breakup, it is one of the primary causes.[1] **"**
>
> **—Aubrey Andelin**

Scripture shows little sympathy for the lazy or irresponsible. Paul laid down this rule for the Thessalonian church: "If a man will not work, he shall not eat" (2Th 3:10). He also told Timothy, "If anyone does not provide for his relatives, and especially for his immediate family, he has denied the faith and is worse than an unbeliever" (1Ti 5:8). Did you notice the pronoun here? Paul is talking to men.

For Further Study:
What does Proverbs 6:6-11 say about the financial prospects of the "sluggard"? (See also Pr 13:4; 20:4; and 26:15)

The Christian man can face this obligation with confidence. Assuming he upholds his end of the deal, he has an amazing promise about God's eagerness to provide: "But seek first his kingdom and his righteousness, and all these things [food, shelter, clothing, etc.] will be given to you as well" (Mt 6:33). Faith in a loving and generous God brings tremendous peace. Not so for the unbeliever. Cut off from the assurance and love of God, he feels compelled to fight, claw, and scratch his way to financial security.

Ask ten men what it means to be a good provider and you might well get ten different answers. One man could feel negligent unless he has supplied his wife with a Rolls

Royce and a fur coat; another could think he was doing great if his wife had a roof over her head—the roof of a homeless shelter. Rather than making cultural comparisons or trying to find the national average, let's identify the biblical standard of provision.

Assure your wife. Husbands, if you aren't demonstrating a consistent concern about the family finances, you are forcing your wife to be concerned. Your irresponsibility will threaten her sense of peace and security. It goes without saying that she is partly responsible for how the money is spent, and that her ultimate security can only be found in God. But for her to have peace of mind she needs to know you know about—and care about—the financial condition of your household. She should have the freedom to give you her counsel without having to carry the burden of responsibility.

Women have been stereotyped as the big spenders. They are always the ones shown in commercials or sitcoms swarming through malls with shopping bags bulging. But that's not really fair. The wife may go out and splurge on a new dress. Meanwhile her husband goes out and buys a new boat or puts an addition on the house! I have to push Betsy out the door and tell her to spend money. She has to hold me back!

Author Steve Farrar makes this comment about the big-spending husband in his book *Point Man*: "To him, it's no big deal. Sometimes he buys new socks, sometimes he buys a new TV...Now if this guy is head of his home, can he go out and make that kind of financial decision? Yes. Is that the wise way to make a major purchase? No. The mature man makes himself mutually accountable to his wife by including her in the decision-making process. The immature man goes off and does what he wants without considering his wife's perspective...This is poor leadership, no matter how you cut it."[2]

Don't be a burden. If financial calamity strikes, the husband should be humble enough to submit his needs to the church. Don't let pride cut you off from the support of the body of Christ. In my role as a pastor, though, I have counseled men who seemed to rely too heavily on the church's generosity. There was one season in particular where a number of men felt it was time to be flexible and creative in their pursuit of career and education. As I sat listening to them describe their plans, I thought, *This may be your choice, but it's going to wind up on the church's doorstep when the bills aren't getting paid.*

God's Word specifically exhorts us not to be a burden

on the church. "We were not idle when we were with you," wrote Paul, "nor did we eat anyone's food without paying for it. On the contrary, we worked night and day, laboring and toiling so that we would not be a burden to any of you" (2Th 3:7,8). By taking responsibility for our own needs, we free the church to help those in genuine crisis.

Give in faith. One of the more sobering sections of the Bible appears in the third chapter of Malachi, where God accuses Israel of robbing him. Their answer reveals the extent of their ignorance: "How do we rob you?" "In tithes and offerings," answers God. "You are under a curse—the whole nation of you—because you are robbing me. Bring the whole tithe into the storehouse, that there may be food in my house" (Mal 3:8-10).

When we fail to give God what is his—the first 10 percent of our income—we rob him and his Church. We take something which by right belongs to another. And we bring a curse on our own finances. Our refusal to give to God restricts his provision for us.

The Old and New Testaments are filled with passages challenging us to give generously, expecting nothing in return. Because we are made in the image of God and are being continually transformed to be like him, we have within us a desire to give. To a small degree we mirror his generosity. If we allow fear, greed, or ignorance to quench that within us, we end up robbing God of glory and robbing others of the benefits.

For Further Study:
Some of the Old Testament references to the tithe include Lev 27:30; Dt 12:6,17; 14:22; 2Ch 31:2-6; and Ne 10:37; 12:44.

> **❝** I view tithing as I view a child's first steps. His first steps are not his last, neither are they his best, but they are a fine beginning. So is the tithe. Tithing is for many the first toddler's step of stewardship. It is the training wheels on the bicycle of true giving. It may not be a home run, but it gets you on base—which is a lot further than the majority of church members ever get.[3] **❞**
>
> —**Randy Alcorn**

---

2 Name one instance when you experienced the truth, "It is more blessed to give than to receive" (Ac 20:35).

It takes faith to overcome the spirit of this age. Society teaches us to grab; God says to give. We are servants in "The Upside Down Kingdom," as one book title described it. Yet as unnatural as God's financial principles may seem, they work. We could devote pages and pages of this book to stories of people in financial crisis who thought it would be impossible to obey Scripture...until they began doing it and saw God miraculously provide.

Without faith we cannot please God—period. And few things will exercise your faith like biblical giving. These biblical principles may well appear foreign to you. They may seem totally unrealistic: "How can we tithe? All our money is accounted for, and the bills are stacked up three inches high!" Before you argue, thoroughly study what the Bible says about the topic. You'll uncover some stern warnings. You will also find some incredible promises, like this follow-up to the earlier passage we read in Malachi: "'Test me in this,' says the Lord Almighty, 'and see if I will not throw open the floodgates of heaven and pour out so much blessing that you will not have room enough for it'" (Mal 3:10).

Meditate on 2 Corinthians 9:6-8.
What two characteristics of godly giving does this passage reveal?

I (Betsy) have married a man of faith who serves cheerfully and is very generous. I have learned so much by following his leadership. He has helped me realize that the money we have is really not ours. It belongs to God. "The earth is the Lord's, and everything in it" (Ps 24:1). That certainly puts materialism in perspective! God "loans" us the money so we can invest it in his purpose. In turn, we experience the truth of Solomon's proverb: "The generous man will be prosperous, and he who waters will himself be watered" (Pr 11:25 NAS).

> 66 Because we invest most of our days working in exchange for money, there is a very real sense in which our money represents *us*. Therefore, how we use it expresses who we are, what our priorities are, and what's in our hearts. As we use our money and resources Christianly, we prove our growth in Christlikeness.[4] 99
>
> —Donald S. Whitney

Pursue excellence at work. "Whatever you do, work at it with all your heart, as working for the Lord, not for men" (Col 3:23). Our motive is essential. Regardless of whether we receive a salary increase or recommendation, we need to work faithfully under God's supervision. And while we should strive to maximize our earnings, we cannot compromise biblical values and priorities. Will getting the raise force you to spend less time at home with your family? Put extra pressure on your wife? Cause you to

Meditate on Psalm 1:1-3. Prosperity is the reward for meditating on and applying God's Word.

relocate away from your church? Make sure that your commitment to the person and purpose of Jesus Christ shapes your financial decisions—not vice versa.

Prove yourself a wholehearted worker by doing the following:

■ Come to work a little early, and make sure you're not the first to leave.

■ Be willing to do distasteful or tedious jobs with a cheerful spirit.

■ Improve your vocational level by taking advantage of every opportunity to learn.

■ Be the most dependable person on the job.

■ Look for ways to improve efficiency. Do this humbly without seeking favoritism from your supervisor.

■ Encourage, support, and submit to your superiors. Try to make them a success.

When we act on God's precepts, we become more of an asset to those we serve. We grow in character and skill. And employers will pay to keep valuable workers like that.

Set your business in order before building your house. Those not yet married may benefit most from this final principle, but it's one worthy of study by all: "Prepare your work outside, and make it ready for yourself in the field; afterwards, then, build your house" (Pr 24:27). We can apply this verse to marriage. If we're smart we'll do our homework in advance before undertaking this major financial endeavor. Do you have a place to live? Do you have a career that can support a family? If a man plans to be a good provider, those are the kinds of questions he should be asking himself prior to getting engaged.

Meditate on Proverbs 22:3. If you're not yet married, what plans do you need to make? If you are already married, what plans *should* you have made?

Now some men carry this too far. You don't necessarily need your little bungalow with the picket fence and a dog in the yard before you're eligible to consider marriage. If I had shown a greater degree of faith, my engagement to Betsy probably would have been far shorter. Just make sure your faith isn't foolishness in disguise. "He who makes haste with his feet errs" (Pr 19:2 NAS).

Being a Good Manager

Providing an income is one thing. But once you have it, how do you use it? What kind of criteria can we find in Scripture for managing the money God gives us?

Accept your responsibility. As head of the house, the husband should accept responsibility for overseeing the family finances. This doesn't mean you make unilateral

109

decisions, nor does it mean you keep a lock and key on the ledger. You may well choose to delegate a great deal to your wife, depending on your respective gifts. But unless you feel the weight of responsibility you won't view financial decisions with the necessary sense of urgency. You won't exercise the foresight to plan for long-term needs. What you *will* do is cause your wife to suffer under an undue burden of anxiety.

For example, suppose I (Gary) begin pursuing a magnificently creative (and expensive) idea for a romantic getaway or vacation, but give no indication to Betsy that I am in tune with the budget, with our current level of savings, or with upcoming needs. Rather than inspiring her, my plan makes her insecure. She begins to wonder whether I am ignorant of or indifferent to our financial state.

---

3 What is your biggest concern or question about the current state of your finances?

Similar tension can arise over our interpretation of the budget. I (Betsy) see the columns in a certain way. We have this much set aside for clothing, that much set aside for vacation, and so on. But for Gary, it's easy to say, "Oh, we're out of money in clothing? Let's just shift some from the vacation column." In his mind, we'll simply reimburse the vacation column with the next paycheck. I'm thinking, *But you can't shift—that's the vacation fund!* I tend to view the budget as a series of separate accounts, while he views it as one account. When his flexible approach and my rigid approach collide, I can get nervous.

It doesn't matter who writes the checks and records the expenses. Husband or wife can do this, depending on your gifts and schedule. But it is the man's responsibility to oversee this sensitive area. By keeping your finger on the financial pulse you will greatly increase the peace of your household.

Get out of debt. It's been years now, but I (Gary) clearly remember the day the salesman showed up at my parents' door offering a set of books representing the world's best literature. I had just gotten home from college, and the flush of academic excitement must not have worn off yet. While I sat across from the salesman, my dad sat at the other end of the table saying, "Don't do this." But I did anyway. For several months the novelty of these beautiful and impressive books, the products of civilization's greatest thinkers, stayed with me. After about the fifth payment, however, I began to realize how long I would have to wear this collar of debt around my neck. It reached the point where after writing my check I would practically slam it down on the table and say, "Here! Here's your check!" I eventually sold the books to get extra money quickly. Now I have something else to regret!

Paul instructed the Romans, "Owe nothing to anyone except to love one another" (Ro 13:8 NAS). As I understand it, this verse means we're to pay our bills on time. Are we sinning if we borrow to buy a car? Some would say so. Others disagree. But there's no argument that the Bible repeatedly warns of the bondage, danger, and calamity that can come upon us if we mismanage our money and start spending what we don't have. As everyone who has had to deal with a monthly bill knows, "The rich rules over the poor, and the borrower becomes the lender's slave" (Pr 22:7 NAS).

> **"** Anyone who ever got into debt knows getting there is a lot of fun. It's not nearly as much fun getting out.[5]
>
> **"**
> **—Larry Burkett**

Take a look at one of your credit cards some time. Do you see a rectangular piece of plastic—or do you see a philosophy? Credit cards have gained such tremendous popularity because they promise us we can get it *now*, enjoy it *now*, and pay for it later. The problem is, we may not be able to pay for it later because of the accumulated interest. Like the federal government, numerous households are forced to borrow just to pay the interest on previous loans.

Credit is so easily gotten in this day and age. Every year we receive at least half a dozen letters offering us new credit cards. I (Betsy) have stood in line behind people at stores and been amazed to see layer after layer of plastic in their wallets. How do they keep track of all the bills coming in? Apparently some don't—that's why there are "credit card hospitals" in some cities where you can turn over your credit cards to a professional who cuts them up and then negotiates payments with your creditors.

For Further Study:
Read Proverbs 6:1-5 and 22:26-27. How would you characterize this attitude toward debt?

It's the philosophy—not the plastic—which Christians should reject. Gary and I frequently use a credit card as a convenient way to make purchases. When the bill arrives, though, we pay it in full. If we can't pay in full, we don't make the purchase.

Credit spending is a dangerous trap. So many newly-weds go into debt for their honeymoon or home furnishings or any number of things. As a result, those first years they expected to be so blissful flare up with one financial crisis after another.

> 66 Citibank calculates that a consumer using a credit card will buy 26 percent more than he would if he was carrying cash, even if he pays it all off without interest charges. The convenience of having a credit card is also a liability—its very convenience constitutes temptation.[6] 99
>
> —Randy Alcorn

It will force you to buck the cultural tide, but take the wise course and adopt a biblical philosophy: If you don't have it, don't spend it. This is a small price to pay for being in God's will, maintaining harmony in your home, and being able to do the other things God wants you to do with your money.

4 For which of the following would you be willing to go into debt? (Check any that apply)

❑ Buying a home

❑ Taking a much-needed vacation

❑ Buying a car

❑ Giving money to a needy relative

❑ Buying furniture

❑ Buying season tickets to watch professional football

Simplify your lifestyle. A study was done which found that the average American couple is over $500 dollars per month in consumer debt. Why? Because they have contracted that dread disease which Randy Alcorn has termed "affluenza." We're not the first generation to experience this craving for material things. Paul had to confront the same tendencies in the first-century Church. Here was his counsel:

But godliness with contentment is great gain. For we brought nothing into the world, and we can take nothing out of it. But if we have food and clothing, we will be content with that. People who want to get rich fall into temptation and a trap and into many foolish and harmful desires that plunge men into ruin and destruction. For the love of money is a root of all kinds of evil. Some people, eager for money, have wandered from the faith and pierced themselves with many griefs (1Ti 6:6-10).

Discontentment is rampant in this culture, and advertisers perpetuate the mindset. There are many who think contentment would be the death of capitalism. Nobody would buy anything. They would wear their clothes and drive their cars until they wore out. God forbid!

Resist the temptation to spend for luxury, style, elegance, or expensive hobbies. Following Scripture's advice requires that we distinguish between what we want and what we *need*. The two are often miles apart. For example, I (Gary) take an interest in pens. To me a pen is much more than something to write with—it is a fine instrument, a craftsman's tool. I receive a pen catalog which lists pens that cost up to eight *thousand* dollars! Now I haven't bought one of those yet, and I never will. I couldn't justify it. It's not a priority or a need. My Parker pens do a very satisfactory job of putting ink on paper for a fraction of the cost. (Of course I carry the complete set of four in my notebook…a ballpoint, a pencil, a roller ball, and a fountain pen in case I ever get asked to autograph copies of this book!)

> **❝** The lust for affluence in contemporary society has become psychotic; it has completely lost touch with reality.[7] **❞**
> —**Richard Foster**

We've found the following guidelines very helpful when deciding whether or not to make a purchase:

- Do we need it?
- Can we afford it?
- Do we need something else more?
- Can we get by without it?

The last one is usually the clincher. Though you may fight tooth and nail to convince yourself of the item's value, the fact is there are few things you couldn't live without.

Meditate on Hebrews 13:5. According to this verse, why should we be content with what we have?

Couples facing a financial crunch frequently diagnose their problem as a lack of money. The cure? More money. But before you start trying to increase your income, scrutinize the "outgo." Are you saddled with debt you incurred for non-essential items? Are the things you are paying for worth the extra stress and fatigue that additional employment will cause? In most cases, the quickest and healthiest way to financial freedom is not to increase your income but to decrease your bills.

You may have pared your expenses down to the bone and still be in need of extra income. We don't want anyone to feel guilty if you are in that kind of situation. In most cases, though, the solution lies in making wiser use of what we have rather than trying to make more. Our goal—and we believe it is a biblical one—is that couples reach a place where their needs are met and they can give to God and others without having to depend on the wife's income.

You'll simplify your lifestyle and reduce expenses dramatically simply by learning to maintain your own property. When I (Gary) was growing up, my dad put me to work doing all kinds of home projects and repairs. At the time I didn't like it much. I would much rather have been playing football with my friends. But now that I own a home, I'm deeply grateful for the way Dad taught me to fix things around the house. It saves us a lot of money.

For Further Study:
Read Matthew 6:25-34.
A sure-fire cure for financial anxiety!

> **❝** Money never stays with me. It would burn me if it did. I throw it out of my hands as soon as possible, lest it should find its way into my heart.[8] **❞**
>
> **—John Wesley**

It may take some trial and error to discover what you can do yourself and what will require professional help. Lots of men do their own car repairs. I don't trust myself enough for that. I don't want Betsy driving down the interstate wondering, *Did Gary fix the brakes or not?* I don't do electricity either, or plumbing…though I had to learn about plumbing the hard way.

Not long after we were married, Betsy and I found ourselves awake at one o'clock in the morning, unable to sleep because the toilet was running. Finally I decided to get up and fix it. A minor adjustment, I thought. So I took the top off the back of the commode and began turning something in there. Next thing I knew, the piece had broken off in my hand and water was shooting straight up to the ceiling! Of course the valve below the toilet was stuck, so I had to run downstairs for my tools and run back to wrench it shut. Meanwhile the water was still shooting up everywhere. Finally I got the valve closed.

The toilet wasn't running anymore, but our bathroom was now covered with water. After we mopped it all up with towels I was ready to go back to bed. But not Betsy. She wanted to scrub the whole bathroom with Lysol. In her mind, it was contaminated with toilet water and she wasn't about to let that sit all night. My efforts to convince her that it was clean water were ineffective. Somewhere around 4:00 that morning I climbed back in bed, knowing my plumbing days were over.

One quick word for wives on maintaining the home. The atmosphere you create in your home is much more important than the decorations and furniture inside. Is there life in your relationship with the Lord, with your husband, and with your children? That's what will distinguish your home from a museum. And while investing in the life of your home will take plenty of effort and creativity, it doesn't have to take much cash.

Budget your money. Unless your financial transactions rival those of a Fortune 500 corporation, you won't require any special training or background to implement a budget. If you don't have a lot of money, it's not complicated at all! The bills come in and the money goes out—a very simple process. For those just getting started, we recommend an excellent resource called *The Financial Planning Workbook*, by Larry Burkett.

A budget is a system of disciplined spending based on your income. It's a tool that will enable you to make prudent decisions and spend money without guilt. But its effectiveness depends on you. If you stick to your budget and let it define your expenditures, you will prosper. Ignore it, though, and it's of no value. Once again, Solomon gives us an applicable proverb: "The plans of the diligent lead to profit as surely as haste leads to poverty" (Pr 21:5).

Meditate on Proverbs 24:3-4. Can you see how a budget will help you fulfill this exciting promise?

---

5 In which of the following areas are you most tempted to spend money?

❑ Clothing   ❑ Food

❑ Home improvement   ❑ Car

❑ Recreation and entertainment   ❑ Hobbies

❑ Long-distance phone calls   ❑ Charities

❑ Other_____

I (Gary) mentioned in an earlier study that I determine the budget in our home. That's an essential way I fulfill my responsibility to oversee our finances. But if Betsy questions the feasibility of my budget plan, I listen carefully to her viewpoint before making anything final. Not only would it be stupid to ignore her insights (which are consistently wise and discerning) but I would be out of the will of God. My leadership doesn't end with making a decision. I need to assure her of the process, show her the basis on which my decision is made, and then lead her into a place of faith and responsiveness. I also need to make sure I'm generous toward her, just as Christ is with the Church.

If Betsy and I are making a major decision or if she has serious reservations, I take the initiative to get outside counsel. When she knows I have prayed and have received competent advice from others, she can trust that God will provide even if she is still not in total agreement.

Save money. If you hope to avoid the bondage of borrowing and interest payments, you're going to have to save. This is the only way out of the cycle. Yet few have the necessary discipline. They make car payments for 60 months, and then are relieved to finally have that $225 available for other categories in the budget. But what happens in a few years when the car is on its last cylinder? They start all over again with a new car and a five-year loan. Had they maintained the habit of paying $225 a month into savings, they could probably have paid cash for their next car.

"There is precious treasure and oil in the dwelling of the wise, but the foolish man swallows it up" (Pr 21:20 NAS). Saving money is not the same as hoarding money. Greedily socking money away for our selfish interests is no better than throwing it away. But by regularly setting aside a portion of our income, we are free to invest in God's kingdom by meeting the needs of others. In our

---

A SIMPLE BUDGET WORKSHEET

If you aren't currently using a budget for your household finances, this worksheet covers all the basic items. We recommend transferring this information to a ledger sheet that you can use to record income and expenses on a daily basis.

Monthly Income: $ _____

Monthly Expenses:

Tithe (10%)	$ _____
Taxes	$ _____
Housing	$ _____
Food	$ _____
Auto	$ _____
Insurance	$ _____
Debt	$ _____
Medical	$ _____
Clothing	$ _____
Entertainment	$ _____
Miscellaneous	$ _____
Savings	$ _____
Total Expenses:	$ _____

budget we have a category labeled "Gifts" from which we can bless others and meet specific needs. That's one of our favorite ways of spending money.

As we said at the beginning of this study, finances can break a marriage. But they can also help make a marriage—a magnificent marriage—if handled biblically. I (Gary) am still the spender. Betsy is still the saver. I continue to view the budget flexibly while she prefers more restrictions. And the interplay of these differences has made us a wiser and better financial team. ■

GROUP DISCUSSION

▶ Why does money (or the lack of it) create such tension in a marriage?

▶ Describe one major disagreement you have had over money.

▶ What does it mean to you to be "a good provider"?

▶ Do your spouse's spending habits make you nervous?

▶ Were you surprised—or offended—by the authors' statements about biblical giving? (Pages 107-108)

Answer to Warm-Up
(from page 103): F. 615 years. That means you would have to make 323,244,000 payments of ten thousand dollars each! (Source: *What Counts: The Complete Harper's Index*, 1991, p.116)

▶ Husbands, do you have your finger on the financial pulse of your household? Rate yourself on a scale from 1 (no clue) to 10 (keep track of every penny).

▶ Are there ways you could stretch your income by simplifying your lifestyle?

▶ In your own words, describe the difference between saving and hoarding.

▶ What is your current level of debt (not including mortgage)? What steps are you taking to pay it off?

RECOMMENDED READING

Money, Possessions and Eternity by Randy Alcorn (Wheaton, IL: Tyndale House Publishers, © 1989)

The Financial Planning Workbook by Larry Burkett (Chicago, IL: Moody Press, © 1990)

LIGHTING LOVE'S FIRE

GARY AND BETSY RICUCCI

SCRIPTURE TEXT   Song of Songs 2:8-13

WARM-UP   Which of the following metals has the highest melting point?

A. Stainless steel

B. Copper

C. Gold

D. Iron

E. Nickel silver

(See page 140 for answer)

PERSONAL STUDY   You've reached one of our favorite sections of this book. That's why it's one of the longest! The principles and practical ideas for romance throughout this study have helped us make some wonderful memories, and supplied us with numerous creative ways to enjoy one another. Yet the suggestions won't do much for any marriage unless they rest on a solid foundation.

Romance begins with loving God. This softens our hearts so we are receptive to him and receptive to each other. What we believe about God, who we believe God is, how secure we are in his love—all of these affect romance. God has communicated his love for us in more ways than we can imagine. He has given us our spouse. He protects us, he meets our needs, he surprises us with joy. And best of all, when we begin to understand all that Jesus Christ has done at the cross on our behalf, we are overwhelmed with a gratitude that stirs up our own desire to love and express love.

Loving God's Word is also a foundation for romance. We're not suggesting that you'll get a lot of romantic ideas by reading Leviticus. That's not the point. As we meditate on the Bible, though, our minds are renewed, resulting in dramatic changes in the way we think and live. Properly relating to the Lord brings peace and order so that we are free to focus on priorities like marriage. I (Gary) have gone through seasons when I was not spiritually sharp or consistent in my devotional life. My marriage suffered in those seasons as I got sloppy with my scheduling, failed to plan special times with Betsy, and overlooked important dates. As I'm practicing the spiritual disciplines, my life is in order, and an ordered life has a significant effect on romance.

> **"** Marriage in the secular model, whether futurist or feminist, is doomed to frustration and failure because it doesn't recognize the true designer of marriage—God. Other people, including some Christians, make the mistake of seeing techniques as the secret to a successful marriage...Techniques, however, as good as they may be, are not the "secret" of a happy marriage. They are not the source of a successful marriage. God is.[1] **"**
>
> **—Randall and Therese Cirner**

The final foundation seems obvious, but is often (and unconsciously) neglected: Love your spouse more than anyone else. You are one flesh with only one person. You need to love your spouse more than you love your children, your brothers, your sisters, your parents—anybody.

Men, it is so important that your wife have no rival. Other than God himself, the only thing permanent in her life is you, especially if she is a mother and homemaker. Her world is always in transition. As the clothes get washed, they get soiled again. The dishes get cleaned, then they get dirty. Her menstrual cycle carries her emotions up and down, up and down. The children in whom she invests so much will one day be gone. Change is her only constant. What God enables us to do—not in his place but as his instrument—is provide a sense of security. Our wives need the assurance that they have our full love, and that we will be with them "till death do us part."

Meditate on Psalm 119:105. What is the best marriage manual ever written?

We're writing this at a time when we have four young children at home. Because I (Betsy) live with them 24 hours a day, 7 days a week, 24 hours a day, 7 days a week, 24 hours a day, 7 days a week...consciously or unconsciously, I can begin to put their needs and wants above Gary's. Why? Because I'm with them 24 hours a day, 7 days a week! Yet it's vital that I understand the limits on my relationship with them. They will always be my children, but my role is to raise them so they will *leave,* so they will go out and fulfill God's purpose for their lives. Gary, on the other hand, intends to stay. My relationship with him should continue to grow for as long as we are both alive. The most important thing a mother can do for her children is to love the father. If you want to raise secure children, live in harmony with your husband.

For Further Study: How does God feel about the apple of his eye? See Deuteronomy 32:10-14; Zechariah 2: 7-9.

My brother demonstrated this spouse-first principle years ago, and it continues to have an impact on us. He and his wife had recently had their first child, a little girl. Someone came up to them and began admiring the baby. Then the person turned and said to my brother, "I bet she's the apple of your eye." Without any hesitation he pointed to his wife and said, "No—*she* is the apple of my eye." May we all treasure our spouse like that.

1 What was the first thing that attracted you to your spouse?

Heading Away From Hollywood

In addition to these three foundations, there are three basic principles we must keep in mind if we're going to succeed in having a romantic relationship.

Women and men are different. We've made that point earlier in this book, but it bears repeating due to the widespread influence of feminism. God created us male and female. We are different—not in worth or in relationship to God, yet distinctly different by design. Because of those differences, your spouse may not think or feel about romance the way you do. However, by combining what God has placed in you individually you can achieve a mutually rewarding atmosphere of romance.

As an art major in college, I (Gary) had to take a ceramics class. I remember approaching a potter's wheel for the first time, expecting to sit down and turn out a beautiful piece of pottery. It didn't quite happen that way!

In reflecting back on that experience, though, I've seen a remarkable parallel between a potter's work with the clay and a man's relationship with his wife.

A potter begins by centering his lump of clay on the wheel. When the wheel starts turning, he can't just grab the clay. He has to work it gently and deliberately, applying just enough pressure to shape it while constantly adding moisture. If he lets the clay get cold, it becomes stiff and unworkable. If he fails to add water and lets it get too hot, it will dry out and crack. If he stops the process and then starts again, he may jerk the clay off center, or he may harm it by putting his hands on it too quickly. It takes time, but if the potter is patient, creative, and firm but gentle, there's no limit to what he can create.

Do you see the similarities? I am to pursue my wife consistently, warmly, lavishing her with encouragement and affirmation. That doesn't mean I don't correct and adjust, but those are part of an ongoing process. Stopping and starting is detrimental. If I leave her alone to grow cold, I'm going to face difficulty when I do begin trying to relate. And if I expose her to the intense heat of prolonged crisis and conflict, her emotions may dry up and crack.

Meditate on Romans 9:21. Do you treat your spouse like a noble vessel in the making or like a useless lump of clay?

Men aren't the only ones responsible for romance. I (Betsy) have learned that romance is not merely something for me to experience, but it's also something for me to create. Ladies, we cannot demand that our husbands fall in love with us. But what we can do is create the proper emotional climate for them so they have no choice!

Romance is a skill to be learned. It has nothing to do with your background, your temperament, or your personality. Now it's true that some are more naturally romantic than others. Those who aren't so inclined may think, "Yeah, it's those artist types with their classical music and Michelangelo. They're the romantics. But me, that's a different story. I'd much rather work on my car than set foot in an art gallery."

> **"** Romantic love is a pleasurable, learned response to the way your partner looks and feels, to the things your partner says and does, and to the emotional experiences you share. It is a keen desire to work for the beloved's happiness, no matter how much effort is required.[2] **"**
>
> —**Ed Wheat**

Romance means different things to different people. Don't look to Hollywood for your definition of being romantic. If your spouse would rather change the oil with you than go to an art show, then working on your car may qualify as romance! Romance is an art that must be developed the rest of your life. Instead of being lavish or extravagant, concentrate more on being consistent. If you're not sure where to start, humble yourself and ask your wife or a friend for suggestions. But please hear this: It isn't enough to have warm and tender feelings for your spouse. Unless they are expressed, your affections mean very little.

Romance can be learned, and it is supposed to be learned. If you're not romantic now, our counsel is that you learn how to be. Whatever that means, whatever that takes—just do it.

Romance requires effort. Whether the desire for romance is present or not, we must commit ourselves to the following actions and attitudes.

Prayer. The best place to start is with prayer. If your heart doesn't pound with passion, confess that to God. But tell him about your desire to have desire. Ask God to help you be romantic, to give you creative ways for expressing your love to your spouse. If there is anything we hope to do successfully, we need God's involvement. Romance is no exception.

Planning. Carrying out a romantic idea takes careful planning. If you fail to consider things like your finances, schedule, or need for adequate rest, you're asking for trouble. I (Gary) have come up with some very romantic ideas, only to have Betsy ask, "And what were you planning to do with the four children?" (Hmmmm—a small oversight on my part.)

For Further Study: The Bible indicates that husband and wife should desire each other (SS 7:10; Ge 3:16). If you lack desire, use the prayer in Psalm 40:8 to request this from God.

---

2 Answer the following questions:

	Yes	No
■ Do you have money budgeted for dates with your spouse?	❑	❑
■ Does your weekly schedule include two or more hours for time alone with your spouse?	❑	❑
■ Are finances available for periodic getaways?	❑	❑
■ If applicable, do you have ready access to a babysitter?	❑	❑
■ Men, have you planned and carried out a date with your spouse in the last month?	❑	❑

Feeling. This may appear to contradict what we've said already, but romance requires feeling. Don't hand your spouse flowers or a card and say, with a deadpan expression, "Here. I love you with all my heart." Making a commitment to romance is crucial, and it must be there regardless of emotion. But your emotions should come into play. At those times when you *do* find yourself emotional, when you are so grateful for your spouse that you don't know how to express it, seize the moment and plan for some kind of romantic gesture. It would be unrealistic to expect your emotions to stay at that level, but take action while they are.

Creativity. As much as I (Gary) enjoy giving flowers to Betsy on a regular basis, I need to make sure this doesn't become predictable. If every time I came back from the store I brought bread, milk, and flowers, romance could easily turn into routine.

I (Betsy) used to get intimidated by Gary, because he is definitely more creative than I am. I also saw my own tendency to restrict romance, to put it in a box: candlelight dinners, soft music, and so on. I've found I can stimulate my creativity by asking other people, "What kinds of things do you do?" With their input, I've come to see that romance is experiencing anything with my husband that I know he enjoys. A few years ago at the beach we visited Norfolk, Virginia and went 70 feet high atop a nuclear aircraft carrier. You may think to yourself, *That's romantic?* (I'll admit, I had some second thoughts myself, especially when the children got too close to the edge!) But it was. By participating with him in something he enjoys, I helped forge a bond of closeness and intimacy. (Though it remains to be seen whether I will accompany him on another of his fantasies—going airborne in an F-14 Tomcat!)

> **"** Couples who place their relationship in a high-priority position have the greatest potential for achieving what they want out of the marriage. Those who do not have a lesser potential. It's as simple as that.[3] **"**
> —**Donald R. Harvey**

Words, deeds, and touch. There should be something unique about the way you communicate with your spouse, things you say that you don't say to anyone else. Love should express itself through gifts, acts of service, and thoughtful gestures. Touch is also a significant way of showing affection. "Our need for [physical contact] is more basic than our need for sex," writes Dr. Ed Wheat. "At birth, touching was our first line of communication.

Meditate on Proverbs 16:24. What's one sweet thing you can tell your spouse before day's end?

124

The cuddling and loving we received was necessary for our emotional development, even for our physical well-being. Now that we're adults, very little has changed."[4] Touching communicates care and intimacy—a desire to be close. It can also communicate that you have an ulterior motive and are merely trying to get your spouse to the bedroom. Manipulation won't serve the cause of romance. Let's seek to make touching part of our lifestyle as couples, not just a periodic means to an end.

Time, initiative, and action. Spontaneity is a great sign of marital health, but we also need to make sure we are planning ahead for romance, whether it's a date night or a weekend away or special activities on our day off. As couples with children know, getting a regular babysitter can be quite a challenge. During one stretch without a babysitter we had little choice but to spend our date nights (Mondays) at home. What happened, though, is that eventually I (Betsy) started using the time to get caught up on my house work. It was so gratifying to be on top of the chores (instead of trying to find my way out) that pretty soon Monday night became catch-up night. And slowly the sense of responsibility eroded my sense of a need for romance. The longer we went without a babysitter, the less I felt a need to go out with Gary.

Once I realized what was happening, I took it very seriously...and we found a babysitter. Women in particular, with their tremendous sense of responsibility, should be careful that responsibility not erode their commitment to romance.

This prompts me (Gary) to stress how important it is for the husband to take initiative in pursuing romance. That doesn't mean going to your wife and saying, "What would you like to do tonight?" It doesn't mean asking her for three ideas and picking the one you like best. That's not leadership. Feel free to get her input, but make sure you determine the plan and then take action. Perhaps there will be a rare occasion when you come home ready for your date and she says, "I'm a little bit tired. What if we just stayed home tonight?" You have to read her comment very carefully. Maybe you *will* serve her best by being spontaneous and having a romantic evening at home. But that's not necessarily the case. More often than not, the house is a trap. When you're constantly glimpsing things out of the corner of your eye that are crying for attention, it's difficult to remain focused on each other. Your wife may benefit far more as you gently but firmly lead her out of the house.

Openness and honesty. Romance demands that couples "drop the fig leaf." As we saw earlier in this book, husbands and wives can be tempted to hide from each other even in the best marriages. The fear of embarrassment or rejection can easily cause us to raise our deflector shields. Instead, we need to overcome our sinful pride with a conscious effort to be vulnerable. Developing a childlike transparency will change your marriage—and your life.

For Further Study:
Song of Songs 5:2-8 provides a good illustration of how the desire for romance can wax and wane.

Five Essentials

Now comes the "how-to" section of this study. We don't consider ourselves experts on the subject of romance, but over the years we've tried a lot of ideas—and learned a lot from others—that have made our marriage more adventurous and intimate. These first five are grouped separately because we see them as non-options. In order to develop romance you should make these a regular part of your relationship.

Communication and listening. Having devoted two studies to this topic already, we won't belabor the point. Frequent, open, and honest communication is essential for drawing close to one another.

Encouragement and gratitude. When was the last time you reflected on the various things your spouse does to serve you? Working hard on the job, working hard in the home, taking out the trash, or baking cookies may just seem like part of the "job description" to you, but as you appreciate these acts of kindness and thank your spouse for them you will contribute significantly to the romance in your home.

I (Betsy) remember one day we had to leave the house

in a hurry for an afternoon outing. When we got home around 5:30, the kitchen was just as I had left it—home-schooling papers and books were piled everywhere. In addition, the children's hands, faces, and clothes were stained purple with elderberries they had discovered on our trip. I might have been able to handle all that peacefully if we had a free evening ahead of us, but a crowd of people were due to arrive at 7:30—and I still had to prepare refreshments. How thankful I was for a husband who immediately kicked into high gear, cleaning up the schoolbooks, bathing the children, and serving them dinner while I got the house and refreshments ready. I deeply appreciated Gary's help, and even thinking about it now fills me with gratitude.

> The word "encourage" means "to give courage to another person." It means "to inspire with courage, to give spirit or hope, hearten, spur on, stimulate." The Hebrew term for encourage conveys the idea of putting strength into someone's hands, arms or body so they can handle pressure. That's a big order. But in contrast the word discourage means "to deprive of courage, to dishearten, to hinder, to deter"...There are so many times when your words to your partner will be the deciding factor...in either direction![6]
>
> —**H. Norman Wright**

3 List three ways your spouse serves you on a regular basis:

-
-
-

Meditate on Ephesians 1:16. If Paul did this for the Ephesians, certainly we can do this for our spouse!

One thing I (Gary) have noticed—and please don't misinterpret this—is that women do things to be undone. Many of the things Betsy does and finds great fulfillment in, the children and I regularly undo. I mentioned this earlier: Betsy's investment in clean laundry, delicious meals, and a neat house must be made over and over and over again. She pours her life into our children, knowing that if she is successful they will eventually leave home and go out on their own. I don't know about you, men, but I would have a hard time living that way. When I create something, I want to create a memorial to it. I want to put velvet museum ropes around it with a big sign that says, "Do Not Touch." I build things to remain. Yet Betsy will spend an entire afternoon making a masterpiece meal which, in a matter of minutes, is reduced to a pile of bones.

For our oldest daughter's first birthday I decided I would decorate the cake. I made elaborate frosting designs all over the place—it turned out quite well (if I do say so myself). Then Betsy went toward it with a knife. "No!" I said, suddenly feeling a strong sense of possessiveness about my creation. "Let's at least take a picture of it." So we did. We still have it today! Aware of my own desire to preserve my accomplishments, I have gained a tremendous sense of respect for the way Betsy invests herself in things that are then undone, used, changed, and ultimately given up. Every husband should cultivate an ongoing sense of appreciation for his wife's sacrificial service.

For Further Study: Read the following verses in Matthew 6:3-4, 6, and 17-18. Do you find a principle here that could apply equally well to scrubbing pots and ironing clothes?

Our expressions of encouragement and gratitude need to be specific, sincere, frequent, and verbal. Don't let this become mechanical or predictable. Learn to be grateful for the little things your spouse does day in and day out.

Courtesy, manners, and grooming. Why is it that at home we tend to neglect the common courtesies we extend to just about everybody else? Saying "please" and "thank you"; not talking when your mouth is full; keeping your breath fresh—these go a long way to communicate care. Courtesy is a sign of respect, and no one deserves respect more than your spouse.

If you've been working on the car all day, don't come in and say, "Hey, how about a little time making love together?" Your wife will probably be thinking to herself, *Sure! Where did you have in mind? The garage?!* Perhaps your wife is the exception, and the smell of Quaker State puts her in a romantic mood. But it's not likely. She will be a lot more open to romance if you are clean, groomed, and courteous.

This principle translates to women as well. Since my career as a homemaker and mother doesn't require that I (Betsy) dress up, I could easily let my appearance slip. So I motivate myself by thinking, *How would I dress if I were going on a date with Gary today?* On occasion the children have come in while I was getting ready and asked, "Where are you going?" It's nice to be able to answer, "I'm just looking nice for Daddy." About an hour before Gary comes home from work we usually have a touch-up time.

128

Meditate on 1 Peter 3:3-4. Though cosmetics and jewelry are nice supplements, what is a woman's true source of beauty?

As the children see me freshening up for his return, they get a clear signal: Mommy loves Daddy. And they like getting ready for him, too! It's a bit harder now trying to get five of us ready instead of just myself, but I trust they are learning lessons that will strengthen their own marriages some day.

One evening together each week alone and away from home. To many this may seem like a luxury—an ideal, perhaps, but not very realistic. If that's how you view it, we'd like to challenge you to reconsider. Every couple serious about deepening their intimacy should have a regular date each week when they can anticipate being together apart from the distractions of the home, the job, the responsibilities, and if applicable, the children.

The husband should take responsibility for planning these dates and then notifying his wife so she knows what to expect. (Surprises are great, but make sure you think through all the details. If you "kidnap" your wife for a getaway and forget to pack her any clothes, it could be a short trip!) And men, if you have children, you should periodically do the work of finding a babysitter. Your wife will be greatly relieved to know this is in your hands. This is much easier in the context of a local church where relationships and mutual support are a way of life.

I (Gary) want to speak specifically to fathers for just a minute, especially those with small children. As you know, motherhood is an emotionally and physically exhausting job. If your wife is tired after a long day or if the baby is fussy, she may not be eager to go out for a date. Her maternal instinct is incredibly strong. But this may well be the time when she needs your leadership most. My thinking is, *That baby has cried before and that baby is going to cry again. Crying isn't going to hurt him. Here comes our babysitter—we're out of here!* I'm not indifferent toward my children, but I believe my wife has a need to get out periodically whether she sees it or not.

> ❝ Intimate *relationships*, as opposed to intimate experiences, are the result of planning. They are built. The sense of union that comes with genuine spiritual closeness will not just happen. If it is present, it is because of definite intent and follow-through on your part. You choose to invest, and do. It's not left to mere chance.[7] ❞
>
> **—Donald R. Harvey**

It almost seems to me (Betsy) that an attack is mounted just before we go out the door. Either I'm exhausted or the house is in chaos or something else is wrong. But I find that usually after the first 15 or 20 minutes I'm rejuvenated. At those times I'm glad Gary didn't succumb to my wish to stay home.

Your financial situation may lead you to think a weekly date is impossible, but your time together doesn't have to be expensive to be enjoyable. Instead of dinner and a movie, take a walk in the park or a drive in the country. Share an ice cream sundae or pack your own picnic. Ask your friends for ideas. Scan your local newspaper for possible activities. To minimize babysitting costs, look for another couple willing to swap child care with you on a regular basis. If you're creative and resourceful, finances will never keep you from enjoying a weekly date. For a list of creative date ideas—many of which are free or inexpensive—see Appendix D on page 166.

> **Meditate on Proverbs 15:17.** The Beatles were right—money can't buy you love!

---

4 Of the ideas listed below, check the one you think would be your spouse's "dream date":

❑ Dinner at a classy restaurant

❑ Hiking on a secluded trail

❑ Courtside seats at a professional basketball game

❑ Watching a demolition derby

❑ Going to see a ballet or opera

❑ A video and popcorn at home

❑ Dancing on a midnight cruise ship

❑ Shopping at an expensive store

❑ Bungee-jumping from a bridge

❑ Other _____

Periodic weekend getaways. It's a standard joke among our friends that if Betsy and I go out of town, it's usually to Colonial Williamsburg in Virginia. We once read an article which said every couple should have a place that is their own—a place you can find without getting lost, where you know what to expect, where you don't have to worry about missing the events. You need a place that becomes very familiar through repeated visits and memories. It's possible, of course, to get in a rut, and the writer recommended exploring new places together. But we have thoroughly enjoyed making Williamsburg our own special place. Spending concentrated time with each other in a different environment is an excellent way to refresh and refocus your marriage. (By the way, as we were writing this book we celebrated our fifteenth anniversary with a trip to...you guessed it! Williamsburg!)

More Practical Ideas

Special dates. If you don't already have a personal calendar, get one and mark down every date that's worth celebrating. We try to look for something monthly: a birthday, a holiday, the day we were engaged, the first day of spring, our anniversary, and so on. Make your year a series of special occasions, even if you have to make up something to celebrate! Don't let these dates slip by. Whether big or little, these events give husband and wife a chance to say, "I love you. I am grateful for you. I enjoy being with you."

Husbands are notorious for temporary amnesia, but with a calendar you greatly reduce the risk. Don't forget! Invest whatever planning and effort it takes to turn these occasions into lasting memories.

There are so many varied things you can do to celebrate. We've gone for a carriage ride around the sights of downtown Washington, D.C. and we've had candlelight dinners at home. Gary and I often mark the anniversary of our engagement by going to the restaurant where he proposed to me, making sure we sit at the same table (it's the one in the corner with the little hole in the window) at the same time. Because we got married in mid-October, we've developed a tradition of going away for our anniversary and beginning our Christmas shopping together. For years now we've watched "A Christmas Carol" at Christmas time. One year we stayed up until 3:00 in the morning to watch the 1938 version (our favorite). The next year it wasn't on TV at all, so Gary rented the film and borrowed a 16mm projector from the library so we could show the movie on our apartment wall!

I never know what to expect on Valentine's Day. The most memorable was the one when I woke up in the middle of the night in labor with our fourth child. Gary wasn't in bed, so I went downstairs...and caught him in the act. He had wallpapered the entire front of the house with bright red plastic table cloths, on which were bold white letters announcing, "Gary Loves Betsy"! The next day he added, "It's a Boy!" You can probably imagine how the neighbors reacted to his less-than-subtle display of

For Further Study:
Read Joshua 4:1-9. How did God help his people remember their entry into the Promised Land?

love and affection.

When someone in our family has a birthday, he or she gets to pick a special meal served on our "You Are Special" plate. At times the menu has included such combinations as spaghetti and mashed potatoes. It's amazing how many memories we've created with this simple tradition. Also, whenever I take the children to the grocery store, we always get a treat for Daddy. With each addition to the family, his supply of treats has increased! (One good argument in favor of a large family, men!) I know he likes a particular flavor of "Jolly Rancher" candy, so I will go to the bulk food section and pick out just that flavor. It's such a small gesture, but things like that really enhance our romance.

> ❝ Romanticism does not always imply a sensational setting or erotic physical activity. Sensational settings and erotic activities are wonderful, but we do not dwell there. Too many would-be romantics tend to focus on these peak experiences and forget the less intense, but equally valid, expressions of romance in day-to-day living.[8] ❞
>
> —H. Norman Wright

Parents, don't think you always need to get the children out of the way to experience romance. Being alone with your spouse is certainly important. But husbands and wives share a unique delight in their children. Something deep is built between you as you play together with them, or simply watch, arm in arm, as they enjoy life.

Resources for romance. When we moved to our current neighborhood, I (Gary) made a point of finding out where the florists were. In our area, wherever you can find a Giant food store you find a reasonably priced flower shop. I know just what time the Giant in our neighborhood closes; if I'm out late and want to stop and get a card or a flower, I know there is an all-night Giant in the Diamond Square shopping center on the other side of town. I've even learned how to wrap and price the flowers myself, just in case no clerks are available. The cashiers don't even question me any more! Also, get your name on mailing lists so that you're constantly receiving information about craft fairs, cultural events, and other types of activities.

Cards and calls. The first time I asked Betsy for a date, I wanted to do something out of the ordinary. That's when I discovered the mailgram—it takes a day to arrive, but it looks very official and is less expensive than a telegram. So I sent a mailgram addressed to Margaret Elizabeth Mahaney. At first she had no idea who it was from and was afraid to open it. It looked to her like the IRS! Whether

Meditate on 1 John 3:1. Would your spouse feel the same about the love you have shown him or her?

you're looking at your first date or your hundred and first, the mailgram is an effective way to go.

Stock up on greeting cards so you're prepared for any occasion. After a conflict. On your way out in the morning. After making love. Always be looking for new ways and times to communicate, "I appreciate who you are and who you are to me." Now you may have trouble finding more than one or two cards you think are worthwhile. (Who writes those things, anyway? Maybe they talk to their wives in those fluffy rhymes, but I sure don't.) If you can't find any you like, make up your own! The nicest card your wife ever receives may be the one you make yourself.

---

5 You see a poster at the card shop advertising a contest sponsored by Hallmark. The individual who can honor his or her spouse the most in four lines of poetry will receive a trip for two to the Bahamas. What would your entry be? (Hallmark may not give you a prize, but your spouse will sure appreciate it!)

Meditate on Proverbs 15:23. If you've never experienced the joy described here, maybe it's time to write your spouse a note!

A well-timed note or card can do so much to build romance. One day I (Betsy) mailed Gary a card at his office. The next evening (he had not yet received the card) we had a terrible conflict. When his mail arrived the following day, he opened my card and then called me. The tone of his voice was different. "Do you still mean it?" he asked softly. That card turned the tension between us into tenderness. Sometimes I will send Gary notes when he is working downstairs in his home office. My children will often help with this. If you want to catch your husband completely off guard, send him an intimate invitation via your five-year-old son. "Here Dad, here's a card from Mom!" He opens it up, thinking it's going to be an encouragement note, and finds it is a lot more than he expected! There have been times when I've called him at the office and as we start the conversation I find he's in the middle of an appointment. If I know it's not a crisis I'll start singing to him over the phone. It's been a riot listening to him try to fake a conversation! He loves it!

Whenever I (Gary) am away from home, I try to make sure Betsy gets a card from me every day. That takes some planning. For example, if I'm going away on a three-day pastors retreat, I start by leaving one card in some obscure part of the house. I then need to drop a second card in the mailbox that morning so that it arrives the next day. I put my third card in the mail that afternoon so Betsy will get it two days later, before I return home. Seeing how much it means to Betsy to receive these daily reminders of my affection makes all the advance planning worthwhile.

When giving your spouse a card or note, don't just hand it to him or her. Make finding it as much of an adventure as reading it. Place it in the freezer, dryer, cereal box, pillow case, or medicine cabinet. Tape one to the steering wheel, or have the children deliver it (but don't expect them to keep a secret very well!). Let your imagination run wild.

Gifts. If giving your spouse a new waffle iron or leaf rake is your idea of romance, you're to be commended for reading this far! Practical items like those should be given only if seriously needed or requested. Romantic gifts should appeal more to your spouse's interests than needs. What does your spouse enjoy? What are the things he or she gravitates to in terms of hobbies, interests, and spare time? Betsy knows how much I like books. If she wants to give me a gift, she's almost guaranteed success if she gives me a book. Betsy enjoys receiving books, as well as flowers and perfume. She also likes getting clothes. The selection of styles and fashions can seem overwhelming, but I keep a list of her clothing sizes and favorite colors handy. When I'm feeling brave enough to face the sales clerks, sometimes I'll even get her lingerie. Talk about an adventure! (Then there's the matter of trying to stick to the speed limit on the way home...)

> ❝ Marriage does not necessarily make people happy. But people can make their marriage a happy one by giving to one another, working together, serving together, and growing together. Or they can allow the marriage to be disintegrated by not doing these things.[9] ❞
>
> —Ed and Gaye Wheat

Meditate on Psalm 112:9 and Matthew 7:11. Is God stingy with his gifts?

134

Outings. No matter where you live, there are lots of outings you can take together if you're willing to do some research and be creative. Contact your state and local government for a listing of area attractions. Airports, zoos, libraries, historical sites, antique shops, farms, hiking trails, scenic overlooks, waterfalls, parks—any of these can provide an enjoyable outing. Several folks in our Family Life Ministries at Covenant Life Church put together a "Date Night Directory" listing over 150 creative ways and places to spend romantic times together. It is fantastic!

Don't wait till you arrive at the location to begin making memories. Start as you're pulling out of your driveway. Use your travel time to talk together, to pray or sing, to share the desires of your heart for your relationship. The time on the road may be the most meaningful part of your outing. It's your time together, not your destination, that is most important.

One of the things I (Betsy) have had to realize over the years is that Gary needs quiet in order to relax and unwind. I believe that's true for many men. I can't expect him to get in the car and be ready to talk about a lot of deep things. I, on the other hand, tend to unwind by communicating. I've had to discipline myself to let Gary unwind during the first part of a trip. By waiting 20 or 30 minutes before asking him questions, I make it easier for him to communicate.

Transparency. We must remember that romance means far more than giving things—it's fundamentally a gift of ourselves. Opening up your thoughts, feelings, joys, and fears to your spouse expresses your desire to be close, to be intimate. That of course takes time, which is a wonderful gift in itself. There is no substitute for spending time together. Most men struggle to disclose themselves like this. Yet they should become increasingly open with their wives about what they are thinking and feeling. Every wife needs to know her husband in a way no one else does.

Uninhibited spontaneity. Before Betsy and I were married, I would have characterized myself as reserved at best. I followed a few basic rules: Don't get laughed at, don't get embarrassed, don't put yourself in a place where you are going to be vulnerable. Just be cool, reserved, and sophisticated. Just be lonely and miserable is what it came down to! There is something about my relationship with Betsy, however, which over time has unlocked my personality. Because I know she completely accepts me, I've found the freedom to express myself in a childlike and uninhibited way.

Meditate on 1 Peter 1:22. Are you loving your spouse from your heart, or just from your head?

Betsy may at times regret the impact she's had on me...like the times we're at a stoplight and I roll my window down and tell the guy next to me that I love my wife. Or when we're in a crowded mall and I begin singing to her—especially since I'm not much of a vocalist. I don't do these things to embarrass her. I simply want her to know how crazy I am about her!

When I (Betsy) threaten to tell on him for the things he does, Gary says, "Well, who's going to believe you, anyway?" Once we walked past a square dance exhibit in a small town we were visiting. Suddenly Gary grabbed me and started dancing with me in the middle of a group of people! I turned red all over, but the kids loved it. Sometimes he'll shout from across the street, "I love you, and I'm not gonna' stop saying it until you say it back!" That doesn't leave me much of a choice.

---

6 Would your spouse appreciate the following childlike displays of affection? (Check the ones you think would be well-received.)

❑ A spontaneous wrestling match on the rug

❑ Pinching his/her backside in public

❑ Skipping hand in hand down a busy sidewalk

❑ Putting wild flowers in his/her hair

❑ A piggy-back ride

❑ Filling his/her office with balloons

❑ Riding a see-saw at the local playground

For Further Study:
Read Matthew 24:12. What could make a couple's love for each other grow cold?

Little gestures. Don't underestimate the small things. Holding hands, the way you greet or look at one another, simply saying "I love you"—these create an atmosphere of romance. Before we got married, Gary and I were sitting close together in his car one day when an acquaintance leaned in the window and said, "Oh, that's not going to last very long. Seven days after you're married she's going to be over there and you're going be over here." Something rose up in me and I thought, *That will* not *take place in our marriage!* I still sit as close to Gary as the middle seat belt will let me. It's these little gestures of love that help protect a couple from drifting apart. (And if you see me sitting on the far side of the seat, please leave us alone. We'll get it worked out.)

Photographs. Keep a picture of your spouse in your office, in your purse—any place where you will look at it frequently. This says something to your spouse and to the people around you about your values and priorities. A couple of years ago, Gary had his picture taken for a brochure the church was producing. When I saw the finished product, there was Gary with a picture of me and the children behind him. He had rearranged his desk to make sure that picture of us was included in the photo. It meant so much to me that he even thought about including us, and then made the special effort to do so.

Wish lists. Learn all you can about your spouse by studying his or her interests. What are the things your husband would take delight in? What things would be most meaningful to your wife? Gary's interests cover the spectrum from water color painting to Abraham Lincoln to Star Wars (the movie, not the defense plan) to Walt Disney to naval aviation…and everything in between. To help me know him better, I've asked him to put together a wish list of the things—big or little—he would enjoy. Now I may never be able to give him a ride in an F-14 Tomcat jet. But I can keep my eyes open for the cassette tape he wants. And who knows? Maybe we'll stumble across an air show some day and an F-14 pilot will offer him a ride! It's a joy for me just to know what would delight Gary. His wish list is a great source of ideas for how I can please him.

> **❝** Discover what delights your partner and then make those delights happen in many different, creative ways. Even the way you express your love to your partner each day can be varied and innovative. If your spouse can predict what you will say, how you will respond, what kind of gift you will give on special occasions, then you are in a romantic rut.[10] **❞**
>
> **—H. Norman Wright**

Pet names. Pet names add a playful and intimate quality to your relationship. These are affectionate terms you use only with your spouse, out of earshot of everyone else. Now I (Gary) once made the mistake of addressing Betsy by a pet name while one of the other pastors was listening. I'll probably never live that down. Any time the pastors are having a meeting and I have to step out of the room, they say, "Are you going to go call _____?" (You didn't think I was going to give it away, did you? Having these guys "in the know" is bad enough!)

Lasting memories. One final suggestion: Have some way of recording the memories you make as husband and wife. Once you've invested the time and money to do something special, invest just a little extra effort to preserve it. Take photographs. Create a photo album devoted to romantic memories you've made. Borrow a friend's video camera. Use a tape recorder to capture your impressions before they fade away. It requires some foresight and planning, but these mementos will become some of your most meaningful treasures.

> Over the years you won't remember so much the things that you purchased, or even the things that you did without. But what you will remember are the memories that you made together.

It Takes More Than Matches

We've covered dozens of ideas in this study, and it would be easy to feel overwhelmed. Perhaps you're thinking, *How am I possibly going to do all this?* You can't...at least not all at once. No one can develop a lifestyle of romance overnight. We suggest you not even try. Instead, focus on doing *one* of these things immediately. Then try another. The key is to start somewhere and slowly develop consistency. Don't get discouraged if something goes awry; God has already supplied all the grace you need.

I (Gary) am convinced God has given us men primary responsibility for pursuing romance. Even if it seems artificial or awkward, we need to begin implementing the kinds of ideas presented in this study. Romantic actions will lead to romantic feelings. Don't waste time getting started. And ladies, please be receptive to any initiative your husband may take. It's fine if he takes ideas directly from this book—that's one of the reasons we've written it! Be patient and encourage him as he takes whatever steps he is able to take right now, even if they are small.

Meditate on Philippians 3:13-14. Instead of meditating on past failures in the area of romance, redouble your efforts to win the prize.

Also, men, be aware that you cannot place any expectations on your wife's response. If romance has not been your strong suit, don't expect an overwhelming expression of gratitude and admiration from her. That may not happen the first time. Or the second. Or the third. But as long as you are sincere, continue to communicate to your wife how you feel. God will help her respond in time.

Let me (Betsy) inject here, ladies, that we shouldn't just sit around waiting for our husbands to shower us with romance. We have a responsibility as well to take initiative and show creativity. By doing our part, we make it easier for our husbands to do theirs.

7 What one romantic thing can you do with or for your spouse in the coming week? (If you are sharing this book, write your answer on a separate sheet of paper.)

You've probably guessed this by now, but when Betsy and I think of romance, we don't think first in terms of champagne, exotic honeymoons, dozens of roses, or expensive gifts. Romance to us simply means being best friends. We've taken what we understand friendship to be and determined, *That's what we want in our marriage.* On occasion we will do something lavish, but the heart of our relationship consists of laughing together, crying together, doing goofy things, or talking over iced tea out on the deck. That's intimate friendship. That's romance.

Romance is to marriage what kindling is to a fire. Have you ever tried throwing a match on a pile of logs? It will not light by itself. You have to have kindling. Now think of those logs as things like covenant, communication, conflict resolution, unconditional love, leadership, and spiritual disciplines—things vital to the ongoing health and growth of a marriage. Apart from these, the kindling of romance will soon burn itself out. However, if you neglect to use the kindling, the logs may never ignite. And sometimes, if the logs have burned low, you need a little bit of kindling to get them blazing again. That's what romance can do for a marriage.

God's ultimate purpose for romance is the same as his purpose for marriage: to bring him glory and to demonstrate the remarkable relationship between Christ and the Church. Merely being faithful to your spouse is quite a testimony in this society. But as you go beyond that to communicate love for your spouse in a consistent, creative, and uninhibited way, the world can't help but notice. God will be honored. And you will be building something into your spouse and marriage for which there is no substitute.

In the days and weeks ahead, ask the Holy Spirit to give you creative ways to express your love for your spouse. Humbly ask him for the "kindling" needed to make your

For Further Study:
Read Galatians 6:7-9. How does this principle apply to romance?

marriage blaze. Trust him to encourage you and to honor your faithful efforts at romance. And be assured that as you delight yourself in God and in his wonderful plan for marriage, he *will* give you the desires of your heart. ■

GROUP DISCUSSION

▶ Try this abbreviated version of "The Newlywed Game": On a slip of paper each woman should answer the question, "What's the most romantic thing you've ever done together?" Husbands should write down the answer they think their wives will give. Let wife share her answer, then husband. Alternate back and forth with the following questions: "Where would you most like to go for a one-week vacation?" "What one gift would you most like to receive from your husband?" "If you had $200 to spend exclusively on your wife, how would you spend it?"

▶ How would you personally define romance?

▶ Do you consider yourself "a natural" when it comes to romance? Why or why not?

▶ How does our love for God affect our love for our spouse?

▶ Do you agree that a weekly date is essential for couples?

▶ What do the authors mean when they say, "Romantic actions will lead to romantic feelings"? (Page 138)

▶ Describe any annual traditions you have as a couple.

▶ What is the most memorable card or note you've ever received from your spouse?

▶ Do you and your spouse have a getaway spot that is your own? (Page 130) What makes it special to you?

▶ How should we handle unmet expectations for romance?

Answer to Warm-Up
(from page 119): D. Iron (1538˚ C). Gold has the lowest melting point (1064˚ C). Which would respond best to romance— a heart of iron or a "heart of gold"?

RECOMMENDED READING
Love Life by Dr. Ed Wheat (Grand Rapids, MI: Zondervan Publishing House, © 1980)

SEX: FANTASY OR FULFILLMENT?

GARY AND BETSY RICUCCI

SCRIPTURE TEXT Song of Songs 4:1-5:1

WARM-UP In one year, how many "sex incidents" are televised on America's three main networks during prime time?

A. 1,341
B. 2,522
C. 4,039
D. 7,840
E. 9,659
F. 13,577

What percentage of those incidents occur between married couples?

A. 4%
B. 13%
C. 25%
D. 32%
E. 47%
F. 59%

(See page 162 for answer)

PERSONAL STUDY There's probably no area in marriage that occupies more of our thought and less of our talk than the sexual relationship. We think about, worry about, or dream about it so often, yet most couples spend very little time discussing how they can achieve sexual intimacy. This is so unfortunate. (It's also somewhat dishonest.) How often have you found yourself thinking along these lines:

I wonder if he has any idea what I long for in our sexual relationship?

Does she know what I really need in order to achieve physical satisfaction?

Wouldn't it be nice to talk as openly about lovemaking as we talk about our budget?

It's no surprise these questions rarely get asked. An overwhelming majority of couples choose to limp along unfulfilled rather than risk embarrassment and possible rejection. But we're convinced that if you've made it this far in this book you want God's best for every aspect of your marriage, including your physical intimacy. We trust this final study will stimulate candid and consistent conversation between you and your spouse as you work toward a truly fulfilling sexual relationship.

If curiosity has led you to look at this study first, realize it has been placed at the end intentionally. Your enjoyment of physical intimacy won't be complete until you've cultivated spiritual and emotional intimacy—the purpose of the first eight studies. Please don't try to separate sex from the rest of your marriage. It is neither an afterthought nor the starting point. Satisfying sex is vitally linked to everything else we've covered thus far.

Sexual Intimacy and God

Any fruitful and accurate discussion of our sexuality must begin with our Creator. Sex didn't originate with the Fall. God commanded Adam and Eve to "be fruitful and increase in number" before either of them touched the forbidden fruit (Ge 1:28). Sex, with its pleasure and fruitfulness, was God's idea—not ours. He is the author of our sexuality. When we develop a satisfying sexual relationship we honor him as the Creator and designer.

The Bible speaks very openly and frankly about sex in marriage. In Proverbs 5:15-19, for example, husbands are given an explicit picture of sexual intercourse and commanded to "rejoice in the wife of your youth." Proverbs 30:19 talks about the wonder of a man with a maid (and don't think this is a reference to ballroom dancing). The Song of Songs is an entire book of Scripture celebrating the goodness and wonder of marital love and sexual intimacy. When Paul told Corinthian couples not to deprive one another (1Co 7:2-5), what else could he have meant other than the pleasure and joy of sexual activity? God doesn't mince words on this subject. Invariably the Bible describes sex within the covenant of marriage as delightful, pleasurable, and sacred. Our view should be no less.

Unfortunately, the Church has not done well in proclaiming the joy of sexual intimacy between husband and wife. It's amazing how many Christians are surprised to discover that God designed us for pleasure as well as procreation. Perhaps that's because some of the early Church fathers viewed sex as a necessary evil. Maybe the lack of enthusiasm stems from ignorance, or is an overreaction to society's permissive and promiscuous distortion of

For Further Study:
Read 1 Timothy 4:1-5. Paul wrote this as a rebuttal against the widespread belief that the material world—including the physical relationship between husband and wife—was evil.

physical intimacy. The media have cheapened sex by reducing it to sheer physical attraction, stripped of fidelity, genuine affection, and intimacy cultivated only by years of covenant love. But Hollywood's perverted view of sex doesn't change the fact that physical intimacy is a biblical, beautiful, and enjoyable gift from God. And like all God's other gifts, our sexual relationship is meant to get better with time.

The King James Version of the Bible often refers to the sexual act as a man *knowing* his wife (see Ge 4:1, 1Sa 1:19). This implies a rich and experiential union, something sacred and intensely personal. Here's where the words "sex" and "lovemaking" take on entirely different meanings. Any man and woman can have intercourse. But to make love with one's spouse, to know him or her in this deepest possible way, is an experience found only in the covenant of marriage. Noted author Tim LaHaye states that "no other repeatable experience is more important to that couple. The partners who relate enjoyably to each other spend many hours in emotional and mental harmony in anticipation of the experience and follow it with many hours of mutual contentment and closeness because of their love. Probably no powerful human encounter cements their relationship more firmly than the act of marriage."[2]

So many couples could enjoy a satisfying sexual relationship if they would learn to discuss the matter. Open, honest communication with your spouse about your sexual relationship is essential. We need to be able to share all our inhibitions, experiences, desires, and needs. What happens more often, however, is that increased sexual frustration leads to decreased physical involvement…and silence. Rather than opening up and discussing what's wrong, the unfulfilled spouse backs away. Sometimes he or she actually comes to see sex as distasteful.

PASSIONATE PRUDES?

In *A Quest For Godliness*, J. I. Packer states we would do well to pattern our marriages after those enjoyed by the Puritans, whose prudish reputation is unwarranted:

"In Edmund Morgan's words, 'the Puritans were neither prudes nor ascetics. They knew how to laugh, and they knew how to love.' The realism of their affirmations of matrimonial affection stemmed from the fact that they went to the Bible for their understanding of the relationship—to Genesis for its institution, to Ephesians for its full meaning, to Leviticus for its hygiene, to Proverbs for its management, to several New Testament books for its ethic, and to Esther, Ruth, and the Song of Songs for illustrations and exhibitions of the ideal."[1]

—J. I. Packer

For Further Study: It's significant to note that when the King James translation describes sexual acts without intimacy, it does not use the verb "to know." (See Ge 19:33-35, 38:9; 2Sa 13:1-19)

1 What's *your* view of sex? Look at the first word in the list below; in the space next to it, write the first word that comes to your mind. (Example: "chocolate" —> "hungry") Repeat this word association until you've completed the list.

- ■ Passion   _____
- ■ Aroused   _____
- ■ Bedroom   _____
- ■ Erotic   _____
- ■ Uninhibited   _____

Not every sexual problem has an easy answer, of course. Some situations are very complex. It may take a lot of hard work to unravel, bit by bit, the faulty attitudes we have, the negative experiences we've been through, and the misinformation we've received. But if you're in this situation, determine not to settle for anything less than God's best. We must allow God to bring our experience up to his Word, rather than reducing or minimizing his Word because it doesn't line up with our experience. Fruitful and satisfying change is possible! As you patiently and diligently work toward change, relying on the grace and wisdom of God, you and your spouse *will* replace worldly attitudes with biblical attitudes, create positive experiences in place of negative experiences, and renew your minds to God's plan for the physical relationship.

I (Gary) have written the next portion of this study specifically for husbands. In the second half, Betsy will address wives. Though we encourage you to read the study in its entirety, focus on what God is saying to you—not what he may (or may not!) be saying to your spouse.

Sexuality and the Husband

It's doubtful Hosea had sexual intimacy in mind when he prophesied to Israel, "My people are destroyed from lack of knowledge" (Hos 4:6). But the truth is no less applicable to this area of life. We've all heard (or even given!) testimonies of people who faced marriage problems due to woefully inadequate preparation. For numerous couples, premarital training consists of a 30-minute conversation in a pastor's office the day before the wedding...if that! No wonder half of all marriages end in divorce. It's an honor for me to serve in a church where the premarital training process is lengthy and extensive. We don't want any marriage destroyed from lack of knowledge.

In order for a man to develop a sexual relationship which truly satisfies both him and his wife, he must first admit he is a learner. The learning process doesn't end on our wedding day; that's when it begins. (Perhaps your honeymoon will remind you of that!) Few of us had sufficient training. And all that "instruction" we picked up in the locker room, movies, and magazines turned out to be bogus. It did more harm than good. Consequently, many of us find we've been married for years and don't really know what we're doing...and now we're too proud to admit it.

None of us was born with a genetic aptitude for lovemaking. The mentality that "it all comes naturally" is a major hindrance to the development of our sexual experience. Our sex drive is instinctive, but lovemaking is an art to be learned.

Do you find yourself frustrated or confused by some aspect of your sexual relationship? That's a perfect opportunity to humble yourself and ask for help. "Where there is no guidance, the people fall, but in abundance of counselors there is victory" (Pr 11:14 NAS). Scripture also tells us, "Plans fail for lack of counsel, but with many advisers they succeed" (Pr 15:22). If pride is keeping you from seeking advice from others, then your frustration may in part indicate God is resisting you. We cannot build a successful marriage without help from others. Men, we must not let embarrassment keep us from the will and purpose of God.

There are at least four things we need to overcome if we hope to have a satisfying sexual relationship. First is our fear of talking about sex with others, whether it's with other men or as couples. Next is the lie that sexual problems or difficulties are abnormal. It's a lie that survives on silence. If we were open enough to discuss our experiences with others, we'd find almost every man has faced

Meditate on Proverbs 11:2. What attitude is required to learn how to fulfill your spouse?

> 66 In the sexual relationship one exposes himself at a point of extreme personal vulnerability. A woman risks her femininity, a man his masculinity, in the marriage embrace. But it is that vulnerability, that willingness to expose oneself to the risk of rejection, that opens the door to maturity and fulfillment. A husband who satisfies his wife and is satisfied by her affirms her as a woman. A wife who satisfies her husband and is satisfied by him affirms him as a man.[3] 99
>
> —**Larry and Nordis Christenson**

similar situations. Third, we tend to be defensive about our skill as lovers. Who wants to admit, for example, that he has difficulty maintaining an erection? Finally, we need to be delivered from the pride that deceives us into believing we know it all. It's far less risky to ask your wife what feels good than to make assumptions and stumble into a memorable catastrophe.

---

2 What is the one aspect of your sexual relationship that causes you the most anxiety, embarrassment, or frustration?

Once you can admit you are still a learner, then do the obvious: Learn! Commit yourself to study, search the Scripture, read the books recommended at the end of this study, and ask questions. If you want to try something really radical, talk to your wife about your sex life!

As one speaker has noted, "Couples who are successful as lovers are successful not by accident, but because they have learned how to communicate." Our sexual awareness depends not only on communication that takes place in the bedroom, but on what and how we have communicated throughout the day. Lovemaking is infinitely more than a technique—it's a relationship.

For Further Study: Read Proverbs 2:1-11. Are you willing to enter the learning curve with the same level of enthusiasm described here?

Sexual proficiency will also require practice. In order to improve, you're going to have to spend some time making love to your wife. This may be the most attractive homework assignment you've ever been given! Just make sure your motive is to learn and improve so that you can consistently serve your wife, not merely a desire for personal gratification. Skillful and sensitive lovemaking is an art we're to develop for the rest of our lives.

Your Wife's Sexuality

The admonition to live with our wives in an understanding way (1Pe 3:7) has tremendous application and relevance when we're talking about sexuality. How well do you understand your wife's sexual makeup? What gives her pleasure? What turns her off?

Each of us needs to become skillful in enhancing our wife's enjoyment. Don't assume you know what she likes, and don't limit the areas available for sexual exploration. If you always make love the same way, your routine will lead to boredom, and boredom will lead you right out of the bedroom. Discover her pleasure zones. Look for new ways to trigger delight in her. Keep in mind that her responses may vary. What brought groans of pleasure on Monday may bring only giggles of playfulness Thursday. Don't try to figure it out. Just laugh along with her. Maybe she'll think you did it on purpose!

As you're preparing for intimacy, talk to your wife and determine her mood so you know how to approach her. Sometimes you should be firmly aggressive; at other times you will want to be more gentle and tender. Encourage her to direct your exploration and contact by placing your hands where she desires. It's not your job as a leader to know automatically what she wants; you're just supposed to find out. And the best way to find out is to ask. As a couple, you should increasingly feel the freedom to discuss your sexual desires as they unfold during lovemaking.

Meditate on Proverbs 1:5. How could this verse apply to your sexual relationship?

Another very practical but often neglected step is to become knowledgeable about the female anatomy. For most of us, eighth-grade biology was a long, long time ago in a galaxy far, far away! There are several excellent Christian books that discuss not only the art of lovemaking but the science of our anatomy (see "Recommended Reading" at the end of this study). But you may not visit a book store between now and the next time you make love, so let's cover a few of the particulars here.

> ❝ The process of becoming familiar with each other's genitals may be an incredibly difficult task for some couples. Yet when this hurdle is conquered, the communication may open up a whole new dimension of freedom and enjoyment with each other that they have never had, or at least have not had for years.[4] ❞
>
> —Clifford and Joyce Penner

Most men think the vagina is a woman's center of sexuality and pleasure. It's not. It's the source of *your* greatest pleasure, but not necessarily your wife's. That's why engaging in actual intercourse, if done prematurely, may be very satisfying to the man but not to the woman.

The most keenly sensitive part of a woman's anatomy is the clitoris. This has been called the trigger of female desire. What function does the clitoris serve? Apparently none other than to experience sexual arousal and pleasure. This gives the phrase "fearfully and wonderfully made" (Ps

139:14) a whole new significance! During lovemaking the clitoris must be stimulated either directly or indirectly for the wife to achieve orgasm.

Meditate on Song of Songs 4:9-10. What new ways could you find to tell your wife how much you cherish and desire her?

Here's a statement you may want to write on a post-it note and stick on the headboard of your bed: My wife is aroused differently than I am. She is much more complex than I am, both physically and emotionally. It's not enough for me to stimulate her sexual organs. She needs my tender acceptance. She needs my understanding. And she needs to know I cherish and honor her, especially in my sexual desires and pursuit.

Women are stimulated by inward emotions as well as gentle and affectionate physical contact. As a rule, men are sexually stimulated by what they see. The following bedtime scenario illustrates the difference. (And don't tell me you can't relate!) You're already in bed reading a book when your wife comes into the bedroom. As she begins to undress, you forget not only what page you were on but what book you are reading...only after the book slips from your hand and hits the floor do you realize you have been greatly distracted! I don't know about you, but my wife doesn't have that problem. She can catch up on reading while I'm getting undressed. There's no distraction!

Our wives tend to get aroused more slowly and gradually. Their sexual desire has emotional, relational, and spiritual dimensions in addition to the physical. And if their emotions are out of sync, no amount of contact is going to stimulate them to a place of arousal. Learn to appreciate this aspect of your wife's sexuality. Her marvelously complex patterns of arousal indicate she is different—*not* deficient.

---

3 Which of the following actions on your part might help your wife get aroused? (Check all that apply)

❑ Sing her a love song
❑ Initiate a squirt-gun fight
❑ Brush your teeth
❑ Give her a romantic gift
❑ Massage her back with scented oil
❑ Wear leopard skin underwear
❑ Praise her for specific virtues
❑ Quote stock market prices to her

(Check answers with your wife...you may get new ideas!)

Motive, Understanding, and Timing

Demonstrating the heart of a servant is a prerequisite for success in marriage. Sexual intimacy and satisfaction must begin with giving...giving not only our bodies for the pleasure of our spouse, but also giving our understanding, patience, and sensitivity. Do not make demands.

A man's sexual appetite may reflect a physiological need as well as a desire for relational intimacy. That need should be expressed, but with a genuine awareness of and sensitivity to your wife's needs. Where is she in her menstrual cycle? How demanding has the day been for her? If she's ill or in some other way limited in her ability to engage sexually, together consider creative alternatives to intercourse, or perhaps postpone your time of intimacy. Don't pout or project guilt. Unless there's a pattern of refusal, an occasional delay in order to serve your wife won't hurt you. (It may make you a little cranky, but it won't do any permanent damage.)

If you feel a pattern is emerging, share your observations and experiences without accusing. Perhaps your wife is unaware or for some reason reluctant. Your sensitive communication and gentle but firm leadership will usually enable her to respond. But if a long-term problem or impasse develops, talk to a mature couple. Get help. This situation rarely just goes away.

For Further Study: The phrase "Do not arouse or awaken love until it so desires" appears in Song of Songs 2:7, 3:5, and 8:4. What do you think this means?

Foreplay and Intercourse

In general, the husband begins and finishes every phase of lovemaking more quickly than his wife. If he runs ahead at his own pace, she will be left behind, if not left out altogether. It's imperative that the husband look beyond his own gratification and strive to please his wife. In the marriage bed, the choice between servanthood and selfishness is like the choice between an electric blanket and a bucket of cold water. Think about it.

How can a man adjust to his wife's pace of lovemaking? Begin by creating an atmosphere of total privacy. Make sure the shades are drawn, the doors are locked, and the children—if you have any—are asleep or completely distracted. Underline the word "completely." If you've ever heard that little knock at the door indicating the Winnie the Pooh video was not quite as long as you thought it would be, I'm sure you understand.

Once you've established privacy, look for ways to help your wife relax. Candlelight and soft music are almost always good for this. And avoid discussing topics that could cause her stress—this isn't the best time to talk about whether or not you're going to lose your job. Hygiene should also be a priority. If you're planning to spend time together sexually, make plans to shower and shave. Of course there may be—and should be—spontaneous times of lovemaking when many of these preliminaries get thrown out the window. As long as the desire is mutual, "Quick Encounters of a Close Kind" can inject a spirit of adventure into your physical relationship.

More often than not you and your wife will need time to build up to maximum sexual fulfillment. This is the purpose of foreplay. During this stage of intimacy the man must be patient, tender, and skillful. Many of the problems in our sexual relationship begin here. We simply forget how different our wives are in this respect. The wife likes to be wooed and won. The husband likes...well, we already know what the husband likes.

> **❝** Every physical union should be a contest to see which partner can outplease the other.[5] **❞**
> —Ed Wheat

A woman finds sexual intimacy most satisfying when it takes place in a context of intimate sharing, communication, and affection. Those take time. But making love to your wife verbally is as important as making love to her physically. Besides, a creative approach to foreplay helps keep your sexual involvement from becoming mechanical. Also recognize that your wife can't speed up her responses or her different phases of arousal. Not that she's any less sensual—it just takes her body a little longer to go from 0 to 60 mph. We must be patient and loving, making sure our time together is "an event" and not just "an act."

Meditate on Song of Songs 4:1-7. What are your wife's most attractive physical features or personal attributes? Imitate Solomon's skill in verbal lovemaking by praising her for those things.

Begin your time of lovemaking with gentle affection and contact: kissing, embracing, caressing, fondling, and exploring. Don't be afraid to try different positions. There should be a total freedom to give yourselves to one another in any way that is pleasurable, as long as it is not offensive to your partner. Continue to communicate clearly as your feelings intensify.

Timing the transition to intercourse—that wondrous phase in which the two of you become one flesh—is crucial. The only way you'll know you're both ready is to communicate with each other. Though certainly awkward at first, communication gets easier and easier with practice. Not only does it make for a smooth transition, but it enhances the act of intercourse.

Your goal in lovemaking should be an orgasm for your wife as well as yourself. Please don't settle for less than this. While the woman's orgasm is complex, it should be her regular experience. A woman can have varying levels or degrees of ecstasy in her orgasm. She is even capable of multiple orgasms as her clitoris is gently and continually stimulated. (That, by the way, is something I'd like to discuss with the Lord. Perhaps I'm just missing something, but I have found that my allotment is one!)

---

4 Schedule a mutually convenient time when you and your wife can ask each other the following questions. Please give specific answers!

- Is there anything I do during lovemaking that you dislike?

- Is there anything I could do during lovemaking that you would enjoy?

Premature ejaculation may bring your lovemaking to an end before your wife has reached climax. This is a fairly common problem for men. But there are many good materials in print with effective techniques for developing greater self-control. It will take some time, effort, and more than a little humility, but you'll have the pleasure of maximizing your wife's enjoyment and reaching new levels of personal satisfaction.

Once intercourse culminates in orgasm, you may be ready to move right on to other things. But recognize that women often take longer to come down from their sexual peak. Don't be in a hurry to draw apart. Continue to lie close to your wife, holding her in your arms as you express your gratitude and appreciation for her. Affirm her skill as a lover. Use this time simply to enjoy one another. These moments of lingering together in the afterglow of lovemaking can be as rewarding and fulfilling as any other part of your experience.

Meditate on Song of Songs 5:1. Ask God to help you and your wife fully experience this level of intimacy.

Sexuality and the Wife

Let me (Betsy) begin this section for wives by saying as forcefully as I know how that *sex is a gift from God to be thoroughly enjoyed within the boundaries of marriage.* A gift? Yes! To be enjoyed? Thoroughly! If God had not intended for women to enjoy physical intimacy, he could have easily redesigned our anatomy.

Our sexual relationship is to be an oasis in marriage. Some of you may think, *An oasis? Not quite. To me sex is a chore, a duty, just one more need I'm expected to meet.* Or it could be that you want it to be an oasis, but your husband seems disinterested. He doesn't pursue you. Well, rather than getting discouraged or condemned, let's seek some answers.

The first step to solving problems or difficulties in our lives is to discover what God's will is for our situation. As Jesus said, "The truth will set you free" (Jn 8:32). God's Word offers insights that can liberate every wife to fully enjoy her sexual relationship with her husband.

At the same time let's cultivate realistic expectations. We can't hope to attain a consistently blissful state of sexual pleasure overnight. It is a learned experience. For many of us the learning process will take a lot of patience, work, effort—even some tears and some pain. But when we know God's intent for our sexual relationship with our husbands, we can be in faith that God will help us and change us.

> 66 A wife may demonstrate her love in innumerable other ways, but it is often negated by her rejection or lack of enjoyment of sex. You may be a great housekeeper, a gourmet cook, a wonderful mother to your husband's children, but if you turn him down consistently in the bedroom oftentimes those things will be negated. To a man sex is the most meaningful declaration of love and self-worth.[6] 99
>
> —Jill Renich

It's tragic to watch couples who are either unaware of their need for help or unwilling to ask for it. Sexual problems generate incredible levels of apprehension, frustration, and guilt. They also cause a lot of embarrassment, thus hindering couples from seeking the help they so desperately need. But the fact is, when you bring two adults together who have different needs, personalities, and backgrounds, it would be highly unusual for them *not* to have sexual difficulties. Though we must not be content to let the problems remain unattended, these frustrations are normal. I have met very few couples without some kind of difficulty in this area.

For Further Study:
Read Hebrews 6:11-12. What two things are required of us if we hope to "inherit the promises" of God for our marriage?

It may take a long time to work through the challenging aspects of your sexual relationship, but don't let Satan condemn you. God wants to encourage you, to liberate you, to help you experience all he intends for you. Ask the Holy Spirit to give you something specific through this study which you can begin to apply.

Are You A Creative Lover?

My approach to this material will be a little different from Gary's, but I believe it provides a biblical standard for relating to our husbands sexually. Join me as we consider the eight characteristics of the creative lover.

She's totally available. Imagine yourself at eleven o'clock at night, collapsing on the bed after an exhausting day. Then you notice that look in your husband's eye and realize he's not thinking about sleep—at least not yet. Inwardly you groan and think to yourself, *Can't he see that I'm beat? He has no idea how draining my day was.* At that moment it may seem perfectly legitimate to postpone intimacy on the basis of your fatigue. But Scripture says otherwise:

> **"** A wife's sexuality, her self-confidence as a woman, will leave its mark on everything she does. It colors the way she keeps house, how she decorates her home, the way she stands beside her husband in public, the way she dons blue jeans and bandana to dig in the flower garden, the way she dresses the children, the way she works in the community, the way she listens to a friend over coffee, the way she compliments the check-out girl at the supermarket on a new hair-do.
>
> There is something regal about a woman who comes beside her husband in public, takes his arm, and with never a word, but with her whole manner, makes the quiet assertion, "I am the woman of this man.' There is a confidence and naturalness in relating to other people that marks a woman whose womanhood is deeply affirmed. The way a woman feels about her sexuality affects the way she relates to all of life.[7] **"**
>
> **—Larry and Nordis Christenson**

The husband should fulfill his marital duty to his wife, and likewise the wife to her husband. The wife's body does not belong to her alone but also to her husband. In the same way, the husband's body does not belong to him alone but also to his wife. Do not deprive each other except by mutual consent and for a time, so that you may devote yourselves to prayer. Then come together again so that Satan will not tempt you because of your lack of self-control. (1Co 7:3-5)

Meeting your husband's sexual needs—and vice versa—is so important that prayer is the only legitimate reason for abstaining. And even that needs to be by mutual consent.

I'm well acquainted with that feeling of utter exhaustion. I can remember times when I would be up half the night walking the baby, on my feet all day chasing the

153

For Further Study:
Read Song of Songs
5:2-6. Have you and
your husband ever had
a similar experience?

toddler, and then Gary would come home and give me that unmistakably passionate kiss. *Tonight?* I would think. *Ugh! I don't have an ounce of energy left.* Yet when a man initiates lovemaking his heart and, to a significant extent, his self-image are on the line. Consistent rejection could well damage both. Remember this the next time you're "not in the mood." Instead of looking at your own circumstances, look to God's Word and cry out for the grace to serve your husband.

A few simple changes in your lifestyle may make a big difference in helping you not to deprive your husband. If you're tired and you know your husband wants to make love, try taking a shower to wake up. A nap in the middle of the day (if possible) will put you in a much better mood for intimacy at night. Because Gary and I have four young children and full schedules, we've found it essential to schedule times of intimacy together. That may not sound very romantic, but it helps me prepare myself emotionally to make the most of those times. Perhaps your situation is different, or you don't feel comfortable making love according to schedule. That's fine, but do something to insure you don't submit to those kinds of excuses.

For many women the struggle to serve their husbands is more emotional than physical: they lack desire for physical intimacy. My response is simple: Right action generates genuine desire! If you are faithful to give yourself (and give yourself in faith) to your husband, I *guarantee* you those desires will come back.

> ❝ Emotions do not and never will sustain a marriage. There are those cold, gray mornings of life, when one awakens emotionally weary; obviously, emotions cannot be depended upon for stability in marriage. And we do not have to be helpless slaves to love or any other emotion that we slip into or fall out of. But as commitment binds husband and wife together through shared happiness and trouble, all the wonderful, pleasurable emotions they could wish for will spring forth from agape love in action. Commitment is the bond; the feeling of love is the result. The *feeling* comes because of the *fact* of commitment through every changing circumstance.[8] ❞
>
> —**Ed and Gaye Wheat**

At the other end of the spectrum are women eager for sexual intimacy, but their husbands show little interest or initiative. That can hurt very deeply. All I can offer is this simple, four-step approach: Bathe your concerns in prayer, prepare your thoughts carefully, ask the Lord to keep your heart right, then lovingly confront your husband. If the problem continues, suggest getting help from a mature and trusted couple. But don't resort to nagging or bitterness—that will only make matters worse. Once you've explained to him your needs and asked for his help, turn your husband over to the Holy Spirit. God will meet your needs.

I don't make that last statement flippantly. Trusting God may be the hardest thing you've ever done, but that's what we need to do. He is faithful.

---

5 Husbands and wives often disagree about the ideal frequency of lovemaking. Is that the case in your marriage? *How many times per month...*

	1-2	4-5	8-10	15-20
Would your husband enjoy making love?	❑	❑	❑	❑
Would you enjoy making love?	❑	❑	❑	❑
Do you actually make love?	❑	❑	❑	❑

Meditate on Song of Songs 3:1-5. Desire can be rekindled by meditating on your husband's attractive qualities and then pursuing him.

An atmosphere of total availability acts as a safeguard for our marriages. Our husbands are continually bombarded by sexual temptation via the newspaper, TV, magazines, billboards, and the women's fashion industry. And though men may be more vulnerable to this, we're far from immune. If you find yourself fantasizing about other men or in any way violating your covenant with your husband, look at how frequently you are having sexual relations with your husband. Increased time with your husband will decrease his temptation—and yours—to look elsewhere.

She's carefree. Men can often be aroused regardless of their emotions, but a woman is not that way. Her sexual response is closely tied to her emotional state. If she's experiencing stress, thinking of all the unfinished projects around the house, or feeling bitter about something her husband said or did, these will negatively affect her participation in physical intimacy. You will not be able to make love freely if you're thinking about what to serve for dinner or worrying that the kids are finger-painting the kitchen table. I don't know of any magical formulas for removing these feelings; you must simply purpose to set those anxieties aside and concentrate on your husband.

On occasion I find myself in the middle of a very full day or preoccupied with some concern and my husband

For Further Study:
Read Psalm 39:4-5 and
90:12. In light of eternity, what has greater
value: Getting all of your
day's projects accom-
plished or deepening
your relationship with
your husband?

will start to pursue me. Inside I'm thinking, *Oh no, how
can I make a transition here?* Over the years I've become
much more flexible (and believe me, it has taken years!).
I've realized that in most cases, everything I need to get
done *will* get done, even if it has to wait a bit. Other times,
if my mind is racing, Gary and I will lie close for a while
with quiet conversation and gentle caresses. This does
wonders for unburdening my mind and gets it racing in a
more exciting direction!

She's attractive. Before I was married, I never left the
house looking bad...but you should have seen me in the
house! I didn't bother freshening up, wearing makeup, or
fixing my hair. And I'm afraid I took those habits with me
into marriage. It took a close friend's example and
encouragement to help me change. Now I put on the
same makeup at home as when I go out. I make sure my
hair is fixed. These things have become important to me
because I want to treat Gary with real respect.

Women often pay less attention to their appearance
after they get married. Yet our appearance is more important now than ever. Most of our husbands work in an
environment where they are surrounded by women striv-
ing to look attractive. We need to look attractive when
they leave for work and when they come home. Attractive
undergarments and nightwear are also important. It takes
effort to look good, especially if you have small children.
There will inevitably be those crazy days when you barely
get out of your robe. But on the whole, we need to attend
to our appearance. This is a tangible and meaningful way
to express love and respect for our husbands.

She's eager. There are few things that will bless our
husbands more than knowing we look forward to our sexual experiences with them. Have you ever communicated
to your husband that you can't wait to make love with
him again? Try it! It will encourage him and enhance your
anticipation all at the same time.

Suppose you're not eager to make love. In fact, you
wouldn't mind taking a year's vacation from this aspect of
your relationship. I can understand those emotions, but if
you're going to obey Scripture you only have two choices:
be miserable or be enthusiastic. Serving your husband's
sexual needs isn't an option.

There is a way for those who are unenthusiastic about
sex to develop their sense of anticipation. How? By using
our God-given faculty of imagination! This excerpt from
the book *Love Life,* written by Dr. Ed Wheat, is so well-
stated that I quote it at length:

156

Meditate on Song of Songs 1:2-4. What impact did this woman's imagination have on her view of lovemaking?

"I am suggesting that both husband and wife must use their imagination to fall in love, renew romantic love, or keep alive the eros love they now have. Remember that love must grow or die. Imagination is perhaps the strongest natural power we possess. It furthers the emotions in the same way that illustrations enlarge the impact of a book. It's as if we have movie screens in our minds, and we own the ability to throw pictures on the screen—whatever sort of pictures we choose. We can visualize thrilling, beautiful situations with our mates whenever we want to.

"Try it. Select a moment of romantic feeling with your partner from the past, present, or hoped-for future. As you begin to think about that feeling, your imagination goes to work with visual pictures. Your imagination feeds your thoughts, strengthening them immeasurably; then your thoughts intensify your feelings. Imagination is a gift from the Creator to be used for good, to help accomplish his will in a hundred different ways. So build romantic love on your side of the marriage by thinking about your partner, concentrating on positive experiences and pleasures out of the past and then daydreaming, anticipating future pleasure with your mate.

"Of course this means that you may have to give up outside attachments and daydreams about someone else if you have substituted another as the object of your affections. Many people who are not in love with their partner begin dreaming about someone else in an attempt to fill the emotional vacuum. Even if it is only in the fantasy stage, you need to forsake it and focus your thoughts on the one you married."[9]

---

6 "Imagination is a gift from the Creator to be used for good," says Dr. Wheat. Take a minute or two now to imagine a romantic situation with your husband. In the space below, briefly describe that "visual picture" before continuing with the study.

She's creative. Study your husband. What excites him? What turns him on? Not all men are alike. There will always be new discoveries to make as your relationship grows. Find out what uniquely appeals to him, and then pursue creative avenues to ignite him.

I am not by nature a creative person, but I've found that creativity can be learned! Ask your husband about his desires and dreams for your sexual relationship and then put those into action. Learn from other creative friends and adapt their ideas to your own sexual relationship.

> 66 The woman who would never think of serving her husband the same frozen TV dinner every evening sometimes serves him the same frozen sexual response every night. Sex, like supper, loses much of its flavor when it becomes predictable.[10] 99
>
> —Joe Dillow

One caution: Don't try to meet his needs by meeting your own. (This is a very subtle mistake.) A candlelit dinner may do wonders in whetting your sexual appetite but may not be what your husband needs to ignite his. As Dr. Wheat says, do all you can to "set up the conditions whereby *your partner* will find it easy to love you" (emphasis added).[11]

She's adventurous. We should each make it our goal to prevent lovemaking from becoming a predictable and boring experience. Although the definition of adventure will differ from couple to couple, let me ask you some questions so you can assess how adventurous you are:

For Further Study: To see how Solomon's bride both responded to and initiated "adventurous" intimacy, read Song of Songs 2:8-13 and 7:10-13.

- ■ Are you willing to make love at unorthodox times?
- ■ Are you willing to try new places?
- ■ Are you willing to try new things?

I personally find this second question to be most challenging. For me privacy is a must. But I must be willing to try! Let me encourage you to respond in some way to at least one of these questions. You may be surprised by the freshness it brings to your lovemaking.

She's uninhibited. Webster's dictionary defines inhibition as "the act of holding back." We all have inhibitions we need to overcome. I think God's will for our sexual experience is expressed early in Scripture: "The man and his wife were both naked, and they felt no shame" (Ge 2:25). After Adam and Eve sinned, they suddenly became ashamed and covered themselves with fig leaves. But in Christ we can again love each other without shame, totally free to give ourselves and enjoy ourselves to the fullest.

What holds you back from fully enjoying sexual intimacy? Ask God to search your heart and bring any inhibitions to light. Only after you've discerned what these are can you begin to overcome them with a biblical mindset and biblical actions.

For example, numerous women worry about what they consider to be physical imperfections. They feel too thin or too fat, too tall or too short, too dark or too light, and so on. But a biblical mindset assures us we are created in the very image of God. Here's the clear message he gives us in his Word: "I have created you in my image. I make no mistakes. You are fearfully and wonderfully made" (Ge 1:27, Ps 139:14). Do you believe this? You must! Stop comparing your body to the world's image of the perfect body. (What right does Hollywood have to determine physical perfection, anyway?) Instead, find security in the *truth* that you are uniquely, fearfully, and wonderfully made! Your husband chose you, not anyone else. As you revel in that fact and freely give yourself to him, what may seem like physical imperfections to you will fade as you enjoy the unique way each of you is made.

I do want to encourage you to take care of the body God has given you. Attending to your physical needs—which might involve losing weight, gaining weight, exercising, or modifying your diet—is a wonderful way to improve your health and express love and respect for your husband. In addition, I've found that by taking care of myself I reduce my self-consciousness and boost my enjoyment and my confidence in lovemaking.

Let me briefly touch on one other inhibition Gary mentioned earlier. We can easily view sexual pleasure as something forbidden and wrong. We can confuse desire with lust, and thus work to restrain it rather than release it. But within the context of covenant love and mutual service, no amount of passion is excessive. Scripture says our sexual intimacy should be exhilarating (Pr 5:19 NAS). The Song of Songs unabashedly celebrates erotic love between husband and wife. Believe it or not, we glorify God by cultivating a sexual desire for our husbands and by welcoming their sexual desire for us.

Meditate on Song of Songs 8:6-7. The NIV translation makes it very clear that romantic love is to be passionate, not passive!

7 Is there anything that makes it difficult for you to give or receive pleasure during lovemaking?

She's aggressive. Most husbands realize there is a lot more to sex than getting their biological needs met by a passive wife. When we are warm and aggressive our men will feel loved—not just endured.

Your husband may think about physical intimacy more than you do, but it's not his responsibility to initiate every time of lovemaking. Look for opportunities to surprise him with an unexpected encounter or a creative approach. You may unlock a greater thrill for yourself as well!

Resolving to Seek God's Best

We have been working on many of these areas for many years in our own marriage. God is usually gracious enough to point to only one area at a time. Yet as gentle and compassionate as he is, he calls every couple to commit themselves to the process of growth and change. So before you put this book aside, ask the Lord, "What one characteristic do you want me to change in? Where do I need to grow in order to serve my spouse more effectively in our sexual relationship?" Then take a few moments to listen. God is eager to give you his feedback.

If God is showing you that you've been pursuing your own sexual gratification without regard to your wife's needs, you need to repent and ask her forgiveness as well as God's. If your distaste for sex has caused you to deprive your husband, repent and seek God's help as you commit yourself to being available. Pray for your spouse and for your sexual relationship. If you've settled for second best, resolve now in your heart that you will pursue God's ultimate intent—thrilling sexual pleasure in marriage.

Admittedly much of what has been included in this study has been very basic. Space does not permit us to address the more complicated difficulties that may arise in a sexual relationship. However, most sexual problems are thoroughly addressed in our recommended reading. As you communicate with one another, get counsel from others, and benefit from additional resources, we're confident God will bring you to the place where you can joyfully declare to each other, "You have stolen my heart...how delightful is your love...how much more pleasing is your love than wine" (SS 4:9-10)! ∎

GROUP DISCUSSION These questions should be discussed by husbands and wives in separate groups. Please share honestly, but remember to share in a way that honors your spouse.

MEN

▶ How did you first learn about sex?

▶ Who has the stronger sex drive, you or your wife?

▶ What answer did you give to Question 2 on page 146?

▶ The authors stress the importance of communication during lovemaking. What might that include?

▶ What kinds of things can you do to help your wife get in the right mood for intimacy?

▶ How often do you have the joy of helping your wife reach climax? A.) Never B.) Occasionally C.) Often D.) Almost always

▶ If you had a sexual problem or question, who could you ask for advice?

▶ From your experience, is it realistic for husband and wife to expect simultaneous orgasms?

▶ Do you have any questions that this study failed to answer?

▶ How will this study change the way you make love with your wife?

WOMEN

▶ Which of these words best describes your feelings about sex? A.) Bliss B.) Burden C.) Daydream D.) Nightmare E.) Routine F.) Other _____

▶ To women who are unenthusiastic about physical intimacy, the author says, "Right action generates genuine desire!" (Page 154) What kinds of action do you think she means?

▶ Do you struggle with the biblical command not to deprive your husband of sex?

▶ What anxieties or feelings of stress hinder you from being a carefree lover?

▶ Read aloud the quote about romantic imagination on page 157. What do you think of this method?

161

How should a woman respond if her husband seems disinterested in sex?

Describe one creative idea which has helped you enhance your husband's sexual pleasure.

What answer did you give to Question 7 on page 159?

On page 160 the author states, "When we are warm and aggressive our men will feel loved—not just endured." What's the difference?

How will this study change the way you make love with your husband?

RECOMMENDED READING *Intended For Pleasure* by Dr. Ed Wheat and Gaye Wheat (Old Tappan, NJ: Fleming H. Revell Company, © 1981)

The Act Of Marriage by Tim and Beverly LaHaye (Grand Rapids, MI: Zondervan Publishing House, © 1976)

Answer to Warm-Up
(from page 141): E. 9,659, B. 13%. These statistics were compiled by the American Family Association based on a four-week viewing period in 1992. A "sex incident" is defined as a scene of suggested intercourse, a sexually suggestive comment, or a scene which places undue and unnecessary emphasis on the human anatomy.

A HUSBAND'S COVENANT COMMITMENT

Leave my father and mother to become one with you (Eph 5:31).
- Have you as my very own wife (1Co 7:2).
- Be one with you as the Father and Son are one so that our unity will cause the world to believe in God (Jn 17:23).
- Never divorce you (1Co 7:11).

Love you just as Christ loves the Church and gave himself up for her (Eph 5:25).
- Exercise headship and responsibility for you (Eph 5:23).
- Love you as I love myself (Eph 5:28).
- Protect and provide for you (nourish) and cultivate you with care and affection (cherish) (1Ti 5:8, Eph 5:29).
- Never deprive you of sex except by mutual consent for the purpose of prayer (1Co 7:3-5).
- Rule and manage our household well (1Ti 3:4).
- Sanctify you so as to present you to God without spot or blemish (Eph 5:26-27).
- Submit to you out of reverence for Christ (Eph 5:21).
- Regard you as more important than myself (Php 2:3).

Always be considerate of you, honoring you and valuing you as precious (1Pe 3:7).
- Speak the truth to you in love (Eph 4:15).
- Pursue personal maturity as I grow up in Christ (Eph 4:15).
- Resist urge to return evil for evil or insult for insult, but give a blessing instead (1Pe 3:9).
- Resolve any anger toward you rather than holding it in (Eph 4:26).
- Love you without harshness or bitterness (Col 3:19).
- Preserve the purity of our marriage bed (Heb 13:4).

Uphold the covenant of our marriage (Mal 2:14).
- Lay down my life for you (Jn 15:13).
- Demonstrate trust and confidence in you (Pr 31:11).
- Believe the best about you at all times (1Co 13:7).
- Be a friend who loves you at all times (Pr 17:17).
- Devote myself to you in brotherly love and honor you above myself (Ro 12:10).
- Be captivated by your love (Pr 5:19).

Recognize God's sovereign plan for our marriage (Mt 19:6).
- God brought you to me (Ge 2:22).
- You are a gift from God (Jas 1:17).
- I depend on you, and am incomplete without you (1Co 11:11-12).

A WIFE'S COVENANT COMMITMENT

Leave my father and mother to become one with you (Eph 5:31).
- Have you as my very own husband (1Co 7:2).
- Be one with you as the Father and Son are one so that our unity will cause the world to believe in God (Jn 17:23).
- Never leave you (1Co 7:10).

Submit to you in everything as the Church submits to Christ (Eph 5:25).
- Be self-controlled and pure, a worker in the home, kind, and subject to you so that I don't dishonor God's Word (Tit 2:4-5).
- Respect you as my head (Eph 5:33).
- Desire you and accept your rule over me (Ge 3:16, 1Pe 3:6).
- Never deprive you of sex except by mutual consent for the purpose of prayer (1Co 7:3-5).
- Look to you for spiritual guidance (1Co 14:35).

Demonstrate purity of heart and reverence in my behavior toward you (1Pe 3:2).
- Have a gentle and quiet spirit (1Pe 3:4).
- Regard you as more important than myself (Php 2:3).
- Watch over the affairs of my household without being idle (Pr 31:27).
- Work eagerly with my hands (Pr 31:13).
- Bring you good—not harm—all the days of my life (Pr 31:12).
- Refrain from gossip and be temperate, completely trustworthy, and worthy of respect (1Ti 3:11).
- Speak the truth to you in love (Eph 4:15).
- Pursue personal maturity as I grow up in Christ (Eph 4:15).
- Resolve any anger toward you rather than holding it in (Eph 4:26).
- Preserve the purity of our marriage bed (Heb 13:4).

Uphold the covenant of our marriage (Mal 2:14).
- Lay down my life for you (Jn 15:13).
- Believe the best about you at all times (1Co 13:7).
- Be a friend who loves you at all times (Pr 17:17).
- Devote myself to you in brotherly love and honor you above myself (Ro 12:10).
- Intoxicate you always with my love (Pr 5:19).

CONVERSATION STARTERS

At a loss as to what you and your spouse can discuss? Doug and Karen Duberstein of Covenant Life Church in Gaithersburg, MD compiled the following list of ideas as a way to deepen and diversify their communication with each other. As you explore, evaluate, and exchange ideas about these topics, consider developing your own personalized communication check-list.

PERSONAL

Love/zeal/devotion to God

Prayer

Devotional Bible reading

Bible study

Christian books

Evangelism

Cultivation of spiritual gifts

Giving

Character development

Study of non-spiritual subjects

Recreation/hobbies

Health (rest, diet, exercise)

Friendships

Anything troubling you?

MARRIAGE

Amount of time alone together

Communication

Fun/romantic times

Spontaneous love deeds

Sexual intimacy

Managing finances

FAMILY

Amount of time together

Recreation

Time with each child

Training/instruction of child

Relationships between children

Strengths/weaknesses of each child

Input from children

Goals

CHURCH

Areas of service in past year

Strengths/weaknesses of your serving

Most meaningful/frustrating aspects

Lessons learned in past year

Development of new burdens/interests

How is God calling you to serve next year?

JOB

Career goals

Performance/plans to improve

Relationships with superiors

Relationships with peers/subordinates

Ability to handle stress

Ways to improve witness for Christ

HOMEMAKER

Accomplishments during last year

Goals/areas for improvement

Ways husband/children can help

Outside relationships

100 GREAT DATES FOR COUPLES IN LOVE
by Debra Evans

1. Go for a ride and a talk in the country.

2. Bathe together by candlelight.

3. Sit outside in the moonlight, sharing goals and dreams, concluding with thanksgiving for the blessings given to you by God.

4. Plant a tree or a rosebush in honor of your marriage; celebrate the occasion with sparkling water and homemade "wedding cake."

5. Go horseback riding and picnic on the trail.

6. Offer to give your spouse a body massage with scented oil.

7. Get up before the children awake and have coffee or tea on the deck, patio, or back porch—after sharing morning prayer.

8. Rent a VCR and a good movie (like *It's a Wonderful Life*) and munch popcorn together.

9. Take a bicycle ride to a park or recreation area. For improving your teamwork, rent a tandem bike.

10. Go to a rodeo.

11. Visit a planetarium or observatory.

12. Take a sleigh or buggy ride together at Christmas time.

13. Share dinner at a nice restaurant and go to a play afterward.

14. Attend a weekly adult-ed class together.

15. Build sand castles at a nearby beach.

16. Spend a few nights at a mountain cabin together, reflecting on the majesty of God.

17. Take dancing lessons and learn something new about "partnering."

18. Go to a hospital during open visiting hours and reflect on the wonder of your child's (children's) birth(s).

19. Get up early and watch the sun rise together. (Playing golf and going for a hike at this time of day can be fun, too.)

20. Attend a high school or college sports event.

21. Rent a sailboat or paddle boat at a nearby lake.

22. Go down water slides or go swimming together.

23. Visit your state capitol building for a tour, but get lost in an abandoned hallway.

24. Take scuba- or sky-diving lessons together.

25. Make appointments to have your hair cut at the same time and place.

26. Go miniature golfing.

27. Get all dressed up and go to an exotic international restaurant.

28. Shoot an entire roll of film of each other outdoors.

29. Meet one another for lunch to discuss recent scriptural insights.

30. Share a sundae or soda at a local ice cream parlor.

Reprinted with permission from Christian Parenting Today, January/February 1990.

31. Go shopping together: groceries, gifts, or plants.

32. Go bowling.

33. Take a dinner train ride.

34. Plan a surprise date: Blindfold your spouse and take her (him) to someplace really unusual.

35. Rent a canoe and go on a canoe ride on a nearby river. Find a quiet spot to read Walter Wangerin's *As for Me and My House* aloud to each other.

36. Get season tickets for the symphony (or travel series, or theater, or …)

37. Have someone baby-sit your children at their house, then go back home and spend the evening in bed.

38. Browse in a Christian bookstore and listen to demo tapes.

39. Take a walk together in the rain, under a single umbrella.

40. Play tennis at a local park.

41. Go on a hayride.

42. Attend a wedding and reminisce.

43. Set aside an evening for looking at slides or family videos.

44. Go Christmas caroling with other couples.

45. Take a drive to see the new autumn or spring foliage. Read Psalms to one another while relaxing under an oak tree.

46. Go to a drive-in movie.

47. Share a plate of nachos at your favorite Mexican restaurant.

48. Go for a walk in an area of town with old, interesting homes.

49. Take a bus or subway ride downtown together.

50. Sit on a blanket at the park, fly a kite, then read excerpts from Mike Mason's *The Mystery of Marriage* to one another.

51. Go to a motel for the evening, but return home by midnight.

52. Attend a concert, especially one held outdoors, so that you can curl up together and look at the stars while listening to the music.

53. Arrange for a hot air balloon ride.

54. Go sledding, cross-country skiing, or ice skating together—and don't forget the cocoa.

55. Take a riverboat cruise on a nearby waterway.

56. Go to a park and swing on the swings while holding hands.

57. Plan and work on a creative project building something together.

58. Go for a drive to look at Christmas decorations while sharing memories.

59. Attend an art, recreation, home, or craft show.

60. Visit the library and find a new subject to explore together.

61. Go to a department store and buy each other some sexy underwear—but don't peek until you get home!

62. Stroll along the main street of your town and go window shopping after all the stores have closed.

63. Go to a nice restaurant, but just order an appetizer or dessert.

64. Hike along trails in a nearby wilderness park. Take a blanket and Bible along, curl up together, and read "Song of Solomon."

65. Go to an auction and purchase something funny.

66. Park on a deserted road and gaze at the stars.

67. Visit an art or history museum.

68. Play "hide-and-go-seek."

69. Browse through antique shops and learn about old furniture.

70. Listen to a mystery novel on cassette tape while sipping your favorite beverage and sharing a plate of cheese and crackers.

71. Make a scrapbook or put together a photo album based on a humorous theme.

72. Plan a romantic rendezvous six weeks in advance and keep it a secret between just the two of you.

73. Rent, borrow, or buy a telescope and drive to a secluded spot to look at the planets.

74. Read poetry to one another by candlelight—perhaps Elizabeth Barrett or Robert Browning—and conclude with a special prayer for the strengthening of your love for one another.

75. Tuck the kids in bed, wait until they're asleep, then have a water-gun fight.

76. Play board games for the evening: Scrabble, Careers, Chinese Checkers—whatever! Order a carryout pizza to snack on.

77. Set up a pup tent in the back yard and zip two sleeping bags together for an after-dark encounter.

78. Spend an hour serenading each other with both silly and serious love songs.

79. Go slow dancing to your favorite music in the living room with your best nightwear on.

80. Try fishing by moonlight. Forget about catching perch or blue gill. Spend time gazing at the heavens instead.

81. Drive to a nearby airport and watch planes take off—or go inside the terminal and watch the people arriving and departing.

82. Order Chinese egg rolls takeout to eat while snuggled up together in bed listening to your favorite music.

83. Take turns reading George MacDonald classics aloud together, such as *The Princess and the Goblin, The Princess and Curdie, Sir Giggie, The Golden Key, The Light Princess,* or *At the Back of the North Wind.*

84. Construct a family tree containing as many relatives as you can remember, listing any interesting, distinctive, or peculiar characteristics for each.

85. Go roller skating.

86. Take a trip to a dime store, buy some penny candy or caramel corn, and share it while

relaxing at a local downtown park.

87. Enroll in a (noncompetitive) fitness program together.

88. Buy a Philips' Planisphere, which shows "the principle stars visible for every hour of the year." Carry an old afghan to a hilly spot away from city lights and locate the major constellations.

89. Go to an arboretum for a quiet stroll.

90. Write a family history book together as a late evening project, instead of watching TV.

91. Go wading along a beach.

92. Visit the city fountain and just sit and talk for awhile.

93. Take an art or music appreciation class together through an adult-learning program or community college.

94. Go out together for a late breakfast on a Saturday morning.

95. Buy some Archie comic books and read them aloud together.

96. Cuddle up and watch a thunderstorm from a covered porch or through a large picture window.

97. Browse through a bookstore for bargains, then go out for tea or coffee.

98. Do some photography together at a local nature center.

99. Be spontaneous. Watch your local paper's "What's Happening" section for unique and inexpensive events: art festivals, gallery openings, musical performances, play debuts, and so on.

100. Go for a walk in freshly fallen snow, then take a hot shower together after returning home.

OTHER TITLES IN THIS SERIES

This Great Salvation. Prepare to be amazed as you explore the unfathomable riches of your inheritance in Christ.   (112 pages)

From Glory To Glory. Every Christian struggles with recurring sins and hard-to-break habits. Here's God's strategy for lasting change!   (112 pages)

Disciplined For Life. Trapped on the treadmill of lifeless devotions? Discover fresh power and renewed passion to live like Christ.   (112 pages)

For a free catalog of People of Destiny's other products and a complimentary issue of *People of Destiny* magazine, contact:

People of Destiny International
7881 Beechcraft Avenue, Suite B
Gaithersburg, MD 20879
Attention: Resource Center

1-800-736-2202

NOTES

STUDY ONE

1. This list of common reasons for marriage was adapted from *Ten Weeks to a Better Marriage* by Randall and Therese Cirner (Ann Arbor, MI: Servant Books, 1985), p. 14.

2. Jean Fleming, "Wives and Mothers: Social Dilemmas and Pastoral Strategies," *Pastoral Renewal*, Vol. 12, No. 9.

3. Derek Kidner, *Proverbs: An Introduction and Commentary* (Downers Grove, IL: InterVarsity Press, 1964), p. 184.

4. Donald R. Harvey, Ph.D., *The Drifting Marriage* (Old Tappan, NJ: Fleming H. Revell Company, 1988), p. 116.

5. R.C. Sproul, *TableTalk*, Vol. 16, No. 7.

6. Larry Crabb, *Men and Women* (Grand Rapids, MI: Zondervan Publishing House, 1991), p. 55.

7. Larry Christenson, *The Christian Family* (Minneapolis, MN: Bethany Fellowship, 1972), p. 11.

STUDY TWO

1. Larry Crabb, *Men and Women* (Grand Rapids, MI: Zondervan Publishing House, 1991), p. 66.

2. Donald R. Harvey, Ph.D., *The Drifting Marriage* (Old Tappan, NJ: Fleming H. Revell Company, 1988), p. 44.

3. Conrad Smith, *Best Friends* (Colorado Springs, CO: NavPress, 1989), p. 111.

4. Dr. Ed Wheat, *Love Life* (Grand Rapids, MI: Zondervan Publishing House, 1980), p. 142.

STUDY THREE

1. Dr. Paul Tournier, *To Understand Each Other* (Atlanta, GA; John Knox Press, 1967), p. 13.

2. Ibid., pp. 22–23.

3. Bill Hybels, *Honest To God?* (Grand Rapids, MI: Zondervan Publishing House, 1990), pp. 56–58.

4. H. Norman Wright, *Making Peace With Your Partner* (Dallas, TX: Word Publishing, 1988), p. 153.

5. Gary Smalley and John Trent, *The Language of Love* (Pomona, CA: Focus on the Family Publishing, 1988), p. 8.

STUDY FOUR

1. Ken Sande, *The Peacemaker* (Grand Rapids, MI: Baker Book House, 1991), pp. 19–20.

2. Dr. Paul Tournier, *To Understand Each Other* (Atlanta, GA; John Knox Press, 1967), p. 14.

3. Stephen R. Covey, *The Seven Habits of Highly Effective People* (New York: Simon and Schuster, 1989), p. 71.

4. Gordon MacDonald, *Magnificent Marriage* (Wheaton, IL: Tyndale House Publishers, 1976), p. 71.

5. Tournier, *To Understand Each Other*, p. 57.

6. Gary Smalley with Steve Scott, *If Only He Knew* (Grand Rapids, MI: Zondervan Publishing House, 1982), p. 71.

7. Tournier, *To Understand Each Other*, p. 25.

8. Sande, *The Peacemaker*, p. 20.

9. Donald R. Harvey, Ph.D., *The Drifting Marriage* (Old Tappan, NJ: Fleming H. Revell Company, 1988), pp. 54–55.

STUDY FIVE

1. John Piper and Wayne Grudem, eds., *Recovering Biblical Manhood and Womanhood* (Used by permission of Crossway Books, 1300 Crescent St., Wheaton, IL 60187. © 1991), p. 35.

2. Dr. Paul Tournier, *To Understand Each Other* (Atlanta, GA; John Knox Press, 1967), p. 37.

3. Paul Vitz, "The Return of Christian Manhood," *Pastoral Renewal*, October 1985, p. 48.

4. Piper and Grudem, *Recovering Biblical Manhood and Womanhood*, p. 36.

5. Ibid., pp. 206–207.

6. Steve Farrar, *Point Man* (Portland, OR: Multnomah Press, 1990), pp. 181–182.

7. Piper and Grudem, *Recovering Biblical Manhood and Womanhood*, pp. 38–42.

8. Farrar, *Point Man*, p. 174.

9. Piper and Grudem, *Recovering Biblical Manhood and Womanhood*, pp. 53–54.

10. Lawrence J. Crabb, Jr., *The Marriage Builder* (Grand Rapids, MI: Zondervan Publishing House, 1982), p. 41.

11. Dr. James Dobson, *Straight Talk to Men and Their Wives* (Dallas, TX: Word Publishing, 1980), p. 103.

12. Donald R. Harvey, Ph.D., *The Drifting Marriage* (Old Tappan, NJ: Fleming H. Revell Company, 1988), p. 186.

STUDY SIX

1. Connie Marshner, *Can Motherhood Survive?* (Brentwood, TN: Wolgemuth & Hyatt Publishers, Inc., 1990), p. 152.

2. Jean Fleming, "Wives and Mothers: Social Dilemmas and Pastoral Strategies," *Pastoral Renewal*, Vol. 12, No. 9.

3. Jean Brand, *A Woman's Privilege* (Triangle/SPCK, Holy Trinity Church, 1985)

4. Bill Hybels, *Honest To God?* (Grand Rapids, MI: Zondervan Publishing House, 1990), p. 87.

5. Dr. James Dobson, *Love For a Lifetime* (Portland, OR: Multnomah Press, 1987).

6. John Piper and Wayne Grudem, eds., *Recovering Biblical Manhood and Womanhood* (Wheaton, IL: Crossway Books, 1991), p. 47.

7. Ibid., pp. 194–196.

8. Roy Lessin, *How To Be Parents of Happy and Obedient Children* (Medford, OR: Omega Publications, 1978).

9. Piper and Grudem, *Recovering Biblical Manhood and Womanhood*, pp. 196–202.

STUDY SEVEN

1. Aubrey Andelin, *Man of Steel and Velvet* (Santa Barbara, CA: Pacific Press, 1972), p. 115.

2. Steve Farrar, *Point Man* (Portland, OR: Multnomah Press, 1990), p. 176.

3. Randy Alcorn, *Money, Possessions, and Eternity* (Wheaton, IL: Tyndale House Publishers, 1989), p. 224.

4. Donald S. Whitney, *Spiritual Disciplines For The Christian Life* (Colorado Springs, CO: NavPress, 1991), p. 134.

5. Larry Burkett, *Answers to Your Family's Financial Questions* (Colorado Springs, CO: Focus on the Family Publishing, 1987), p. 80

6. Alcorn, *Money, Possessions, and Eternity*, p. 325.

7. Quoted in Alcorn, *Money, Possessions, and Eternity*, p. 49.

8. Quoted in Alcorn, *Money, Possessions, and Eternity*, p. 225.

STUDY EIGHT

1. Randall and Therese Cirner, *Ten Weeks to a Better Marriage* (Ann Arbor, MI: Servant Books, 1985), p. 19.

2. Dr. Ed Wheat, *Love Life* (Grand Rapids, MI: Zondervan Publishing House, 1980), p. 87.

3. Donald R. Harvey, Ph.D., *The Drifting Marriage* (Old Tappan, NJ: Fleming H. Revell Company, 1988), pp. 116–117.

4. Wheat, *Love Life*, p. 136.

5. Nina Combs, *Redbook*, July 1986.

6. H. Norman Wright, *Making Peace With Your Partner* (Dallas, TX: Word Publishing, 1988), p. 177.

7. Donald R. Harvey, Ph.D., *The Spiritually Intimate Marriage* (Old Tappan, NJ: Fleming H. Revell Company, 1991), p. 84.

8. H. Norman Wright, *Holding On To Romance* (Ventura, CA: Regal Books, 1992), pp. 34–35.

9. Dr. Ed Wheat and Gaye Wheat, *Intended For Pleasure* (Old Tappan, NJ: Fleming H. Revell Company, 1981), p. 37.

10. Wright, *Holding On To Romance*, pp. 40–41.

STUDY NINE

1. J. I. Packer, *A Quest For Godliness* (Wheaton, IL: Good News Publishers, 1990), p. 263.

2. Tim LaHaye, *The Act of Marriage* (Grand Rapids, MI; Zondervan Publishing House, 1976), p. 43.

3. Larry and Nordis Christenson, *The Christian Couple* (Minneapolis, MN: Bethany Fellowship, 1977), p. 59.

4. Clifford and Joyce Penner, *The Gift of Sex* (Dallas, TX: Word Publishing, 1981), pp. 71–72.

5. Dr. Ed Wheat and Gaye Wheat, *Intended For Pleasure* (Old Tappan, NJ: Fleming H. Revell Company, 1977), p. 82.

6. Jill Renich, *To Have and To Hold* (Grand Rapids, MI: Zondervan Publishing House, 1972), p. 62.

7. Christenson, *The Christian Couple,* p. 40.

8. Wheat and Wheat, *Intended For Pleasure*, p. 37.

9. Dr. Ed Wheat, *Love Life* (Grand Rapids, MI: Zondervan Publishing House, 1980), p. 89

10. Joseph C. Dillow, *Solomon on Sex* (Nashville, TN: Thomas Nelson, Inc., 1977)

11. Wheat, *Love Life*, p. 92.